PRAISE FOR
17 MINUTES TO YOUR DREAM

"This fast-moving book gives you a proven, practical formula that shows you how to set and achieve any goal that you can set for yourself. Save yourself years of hard work in becoming wealthy, starting today."

BRIAN TRACY, AUTHOR OF *MAXIMUM ACHIEVEMENT*

"*17 Minutes To Your Dream* is not another get-rich-quick scheme or book from another wannabe. In a global market space today, whereby everyone with a finger believes they are an author or blogger and everyone with a mouth believes they are a podcaster or speaker, Darren LaCroix is a true legitimate proven champion with the mental scars and physical calluses to prove and demonstrate how you too can unleash your dreams with proven simple strategies, to unlock your next breakthrough to greatness."

DR. JEFFREY MAGEE, CMC, CBE, CSP, PDM

"As a dreamer, speaker, author, and publisher myself, I am constantly combing the world looking for success stories of other dreamers that inspire, overcome adversity, achieve the impossible, and exemplify the best of the human potential. In this magnificent read, Darren captures the commonalities between all that dream, and ultimately achieve their biggest dreams. If you are one that desires to tap into the greater potential inside of you and become unstoppable, read this book! It's a game changer."

CHAD HYMAS, BESTSELLING AUTHOR OF *DOING WHAT MUST BE DONE* AND GLOBAL SPEAKER

"Isn't it interesting these three words are so similar: authentic, authority, and author? There are many aspects I love in the new book, *17 Minutes To Your Dream* from Darren LaCroix. What thrills me most is that the author reveals his personal pitfalls and individual improvements in such an authentic manner that you know beyond any doubt he's an extraordinary authority on the subject of success. He invites you to be "all in" on your dream—and I am all in on this remarkable book."

SCOTT MCKAIN, CSP, CPAE, AUTHOR OF FOUR #1 BUSINESS
BESTSELLERS ON AMAZON

"Darren LaCroix has done it again. Not only is he a world champion speaker, he is a world class writer with this inspiring message in *17 Minutes To Your Dream*. It is a blueprint on how to achieve your goals. Don't wait another minute, read this book to achieve what you want in life!"

MARILYN SHERMAN, CSP, CPAE HALL OF FAME SPEAKER, AND
FRONT-ROW LEADERSHIP EXPERT

"'A dream is a wish your heart makes...' We have heard that ever since the Disney *Cinderella* song taught us not to give up. A wish your heart makes transcends any wish your head would make. It has passion and power to change your life. This book will reignite your dreams, and it will show you how to make them real.

Darren shares his personal journey, both physical and emotional. He tells you the truth and you can do it too. Plus, you are going to *love* the story about where seventeen came from. What a great lesson that is. Don't read this book, devour it and then live it!"

JIM CATHCART, CSP, CPAE HALL OF FAME SPEAKER, AND
AUTHOR OF TWENTY-ONE BOOKS

"In your hands your hold the keys to your kingdom. If you have a dream that died or has been put on hold, I encourage you to devour Darren's book. It is real, at times raw, and reveals what you need to know and do to achieve more. You can turn your life into an adventure and get more of what you really want—if you read carefully and take action on the ideas in front of you. Count me a fan."

MARK LEBLANC, CSP, AUTHOR OF *NEVER BE THE SAME* AND *GROWING YOUR BUSINESS!*

"In this compelling book, Darren shows exactly how to take your dreams and make them a reality—in 17 minutes—period! It is not a must read—It is a must do!"

SAM SILVERSTEIN, CSP, CPAE, AUTHOR OF *NO MORE EXCUSES* AND *I AM ACCOUNTABLE*, FOUNDER AND CEO, THE ACCOUNTABILITY INSTITUTE

"This book is a game changer for anyone that reads it. It will change the trajectory your life is on. LaCroix has been living his dream and now shares how anyone else can."

JOHN R. DiJULIUS III, AUTHOR OF *THE RELATIONSHIP ECONOMY*

"I wish I read this book years ago. It would have saved me a ton of time and heart ache. Reading this book is a no-brainer for anybody who wants to do, be, and think better. It's a well-written, easy, and fast read. Do yourself a favor and dig in. LaCroix has served up some juicy secrets for success on a silver platter."

BRAD MONTGOMERY, CSP, CPAE HALL OF FAME SPEAKER

"Inspiring! Relevant! Actionable! It is time to dream again and I mean *dream big*. Darren LaCroix shows us how in his new book. His Seventeen Minute Mission provides a clear strategy for new results. I have seen LaCroix help people enjoy real breakthroughs. If you are ready for hope, breakthrough, and path forward *read this book!*"

DAVID HORSAGER, MA, CSP, CPAE HALL OF FAME SPEAKER, CEO OF TRUST EDGE LEADERSHIP INSTITUTE, BESTSELLING AUTHOR OF *THE TRUST EDGE*

"Darren LaCroix is one of the most brilliant and funniest speakers on the planet and now he shares his secrets for success for any and everyone to pick up and read and grow. Read this book, then re-read it, then tell everyone in your network to get a copy and read it, because your network determines your net-worth and this book will help you all to grow and succeed at another level."

DR. WILLIE JOLLEY, CSP, CPAE HALL OF FAME SPEAKER, SIRIUS XM AND SYNDICATED RADIO SHOW HOST AND BESTSELLING AUTHOR OF *A SETBACK IS A SETUP FOR A COMEBACK AND AN ATTITUDE OF EXCELLENCE*

"Darren is one of the rare people who achieved a huge dream. He also has been a mentor to people like me who has helped me achieve mine. Read this book and follow the advice and you will achieve yours."

RORY VADEN, *NEW YORK TIMES* BESTSELLING AUTHOR, CSP, AND CPAE HALL OF FAME SPEAKER

17 MINUTES TO YOUR DREAM

How to Get the Breakthroughs You Need

DARREN LaCROIX

INDIE BOOKS
INTERNATIONAL

17 Minutes To Your Dream™ is a pending trademark of Darren LaCroix

Humor Boot Camp® is a registered trademark of The Humor Institute

Cover designed by: Aaftab Sheikh, #aafidesigns
Interior designed by Steve Plummer, SPBookDesign.com

ISBN-13: 978-1-952233-92-0
ISBN Hardback: 978-1-952233-94-4
Library of Congress Control Number: 2022901305

INDIE BOOKS INTERNATIONAL®, INC.
2424 VISTA WAY, SUITE 316
OCEANSIDE, CA 92054
www.indiebooksintl.com

I dedicate this book to the eight-year-old dreamer
inside of you.

And to Mom and Dad, who, despite telling them
about my crazy, ridiculous dream that made no
logical sense, loved me anyway.

CONTENTS

BY MARK LEBLANC, CSP

IN YOUR HANDS you hold the keys to your kingdom. Whatever you need, whatever you want and whatever you dream about is within your grasp – if you adopt a new way of thinking, making decisions and acting. Darren shares a unique philosophy with proven-to-work practices, strategies, ideas, and tactics. In fact, his approach lies in the number seventeen. It is nothing short of astounding and can immediately impact your work, career, and life, starting right now.

In seventeen seconds, you can take a deep breath.

In seventeen minutes, you can exercise, organize, and execute.

In seventeen hours, you can feel the difference.

In seventeen days, you can experience momentum.

In seventeen months, you can transform your life.

In seventeen years, you'll be so glad you followed Darren's advice seventeen years ago!

I once read a saying that suggests a year from now, you will have wished you started today. When you make decisions and take steps, however small, and string the steps together like a strand of pearls – you can achieve anything your heart desires.

Darren is a rare individual indeed and it has been an honor to get to know him through the years. It is a privilege to get a first read of this book. My hope is your read carefully, take good notes, make smart decisions, and get to work. Repeat. Repeat. Succeed!

It is not for the faint of heart. The stories and strategies revealed in this book will hold up a mirror to what you will do or will not do, in moving forward in the direction of your dream. Unfortunately, many will read a chapter or two and set it aside for a rainy day. I hope you will devour this book and refer to it often. The genius is in its simplicity, accessibility, and street-smart approach to making something great happen in your life and work. Lay down a foundation for your potential to emerge and you will flourish in every part of your world.

If you ever get a change to meet Darren and hear him speak, you will never be the same. Countless thousands and hundreds of thousands of people from around the world and all walks of life have felt his presence and become more impactful because of his expertise. If you are a meeting planner or executive looking for a message that will impact your people and generations to come, book Darren to speak. You will be glad you did, and your people will thank you.

Mark LeBlanc, CSP

Author of *Never Be the Same* and *Growing Your Business!*

Minneapolis, Minnesota

REAL QUICK—WHAT THIS BOOK IS *NOT*

Y<small>OU HAVE A</small> dream.

You've been thinking about it. Wanting it. But it's not happening.

You've read other books that seem to make sense; but still, you are not in the process of making it happen.

What if you're still just thinking about your dream in a year? Five years? Ten? What if you keep putting it off and miss out entirely on living your dream? Regrets suck.

It's time to finally make it happen. This book is going to help you. Now, let me tell you right up front:

- You've probably read books on the power of goal setting; *this is not that book.*

- You may have read a book on the science of goal setting; *this is not that book.*

What's the difference? This book is going to be insanely practical, simple, and doable.

You'll even hear directly from six of my students who put this to the test. They'll tell you how they're getting breakthroughs because they dove into this strategy.

If you're thinking about purchasing this book or have already bought it, your goal is not to read a book. You want a breakthrough. You *need* a breakthrough. Reading this book alone will not get you closer to your dream. What will? Reading this book *and* putting in the minutes. I suggest seventeen minutes to apply what you've read. That's a recipe for a breakthrough. That will change everything. And you can do that.

My two speaking coaches: World Champion Mark
Brown (left) and David McIlhenny (right)

Striving to become a world-class professional speaker, I got a coach in 2001 for the first time in my career. Dave McIlhenny coached me in the World Championship of Public Speaking competition. Dave had made it to the semi-finals out of 35,000 contestants. After he helped me achieve that same level in the speech contest, he said something to me that was a game-changer. On June 9, 2001, I had won and was about to compete in the World Championship finals. Dave and I stood in the ballroom of the Marriott in Farmington, Connecticut, as the excitement of winning the semi-finals faded and I caught my breath. Dave turned to me and said, "I can't take you where I have not been."

He then introduced me to my next coach, World Champion speaker Mark Brown who had been there and won that. You'll hear more about what I learned from Mark in an upcoming chapter. Your life experience to date is your foundation. Your past wins are assets. Your past failures are assets. I wrote this book to help you capitalize on what you have, good and bad, and take you to where you have not been.

So, are you ready?

Let's go!

CHAPTER 1:

WISDOM FROM CLYDE YOUR GUIDE

Picture this. You are on a tour boat in the Everglades. You can smell the saltwater as you feel the breeze off the water on your face. The sky is blue with puffy white clouds, and the other nine people in the boat are pointing to new scenery popping up all around you. You are enjoying this with a big smile on your face. Seaworn Clyde is your guide. He has confidence and character. His quirky personality has your group laughing.

You are cruising along at a good clip. You notice the giggle of a young eight-year-old boy up front who's having more fun than anyone. He has his left hand over the edge of the boat, skimming the top of the water. He loves it.

Just then, Clyde pulls back on the throttle, and the boat eases up. He makes his way to the front of the boat and pulls out his trusty knife. Clyde leans over the edge of the boat and clips off a large blade of grass between his knife and thumb. He

1

carefully motions to the young boy to gently touch the grass he just clipped. You see the young boy with his big brown eyes wide open and utterly focused as water drips from his little fingers down his arm. Then you see the young boy curiously and carefully touch the grass. He quickly recoils and turns to his parents in surprise, "Ouch!" What the boy thought was grass was sawgrass. The sharp serrated edges of the grass made hanging his hand in the water far more dangerous than he realized.

Without a word, Clyde makes his way back to his perch, and the tour continues. You look back and notice the boy now safely keeps his hands inside the boat. In just a moment, the experience of touching the sawgrass taught him so much.

You and I both know that if Clyde asked the young boy to keep his hands inside the boat, it would have been short-lived. In just a few minutes, the boy would have had his hands back in the water for sure. Why? He's a kid.

So are we.

We easily forget lessons we hear, and they can't compare to those we experience. Experience is the best teacher. We can listen to other people's guidance and get direction. But it's when we gain our own experience that the lesson sticks and carries us further in the direction we want to go.

Experience leads to breakthroughs.

Clyde knew what he was doing. He had wisdom. And we must gain as much wisdom as we can—wisdom from experience. We must touch the sawgrass, often, on the way to achieving our dream. Experience is the greatest teacher.

When I started in standup comedy back in 1992, I sought out the best mentors and was a sponge. The cool thing I had going for me is that I knew I didn't know. That is a huge plus. Ego can make dream achievement slower and more challenging than it needs to be. My mentors in the comedy world all agreed that stage time was critical to my growth. Other aspects, such as writing, are important, just not the *most* important. In fact, Dave Fitzgerald told me, "Any day you don't get on stage is a day you don't grow."

What's critical is the time you're doing the critical thing. It's that experience that drives your breakthroughs. Writing jokes is important, but unless you get on stage and perform them, you have writing breakthroughs, not performance break-throughs. If you are in sales, it's the time you are reaching out to people, facing possible rejection that is the critical "sawgrass" time. Experience, including experiencing failure, leads to breakthroughs.

WHEN EXPERIENCE HAPPENS, BREAKTHROUGHS HAPPEN.

To get from where we are now to that dream accomplished, we need more *"sawgrass moments."* Some of those experiences may cause bumps and bruises; others will be thrilling. They may all lead to breakthroughs.

I'm delighted you are reading this book. I'll be even more excited to hear what you do with it. You might be thinking, "What does this have to do with seventeen minutes to my dream?" More than you may think. We will get to what the 17 Minutes strategy is, I promise. We need a few chapters to lay the foundation for it. Bear with me. We will get to it.

17 YOUR SEVENTEEN-MINUTE MISSION

▶ Experience leads to breakthroughs.

▶ Where do you need more experience to get the breakthroughs you need?

▶ Consider starting a list with the experiences you may need to make your dream happen.

CHAPTER 2:

WHAT DO YOU REALLY WANT?

R EADY FOR THE big question?
You don't have to tell me or anyone else, but you have to be honest with yourself.

What do you really want?

There was a reason you bought this book. There is some dream deep down in your heart, begging for you to bring it to life. Only you can make that happen, but you don't have to do it alone. This book will show you that if you play full out, people will want to help you, even people you may not know.

This book is not titled *17 Minutes To Crossing Something Off Your Task List*. Now, it could help with that, for sure, but that's not the reason that you decided to pick up this book. What is it you want? How do you want to live? What do you want in your life?

Is your dream to:

- Start your own business and quit your day job?

- Have more peace in your life?

- Have financial freedom?

- Find your soul mate?

- Become a highly paid expert?

- Be a professional speaker?

- Write that book you've been thinking about for years?

For the record, this book is that for me. The concept first came to me in 2013. I tried to prove its validity and stopped. The idea continued to percolate. In 2021, I created a keynote about the subject, and several of my students put the idea to the test. It helped them get the breakthroughs they wanted. They also got some breakthroughs they didn't even know they needed. A few weeks later, I finally decided. Along with some divine inspiration, I sat down and made it happen. Seventeen days later, I finished the draft. I can't imagine how many more people I could have helped if I decided back in 2013.

Decide.

Get clear first. If you aren't sure, have conversations with your positive, inspiring friends. You might even consider recording those conversations with their permission. You may strike gold during that conversation and you want to capture it.

What do you really want?

More importantly, *why* do you want it? Getting clarity on your why will go a long way as a reminder on those tough, "What the heck was I thinking?" days. There will be some of them along the way. Don't worry. You are not alone. They are just little tests to see if you are committed or not. Back in 2013, I would have written the book for myself. I've grown up a bit since then and got clearer on my why. Now my why was to write it for you.

You may have seen Simon Sinek's famous TEDx Talk: "Start with Your Why: How Great Leaders Inspire Action." If you haven't, today would be a good time to watch it. In fact, I'm cool if you put this book down and check it out now. Here is the link: https://www.ted.com/talks/simon_sinek_how_great_leaders_ inspire_action. If you have seen it already, consider watching it again. You are now in a different place in your journey than you were then.

One of my friends and coaches is Jennifer Leone from Sydney, Australia. Every world-class speaker coach has a ninja skill. Her ninja skill is digging your why out of you. She keeps asking probing questions until she hits that vein of truth or pain. I've sat at her kitchen table as she drilled down into one of my story ideas, and within minutes, I was blubbering. She found the deeper meaning in my story. When you find that clarity, it can be a supernatural force, pushing you boldly toward your dream.

Many of us seek approval from someone in our lives. For me, it was my dad and big brother. Though I was not completely aware of it at the time, eventually, I understood what motivated me. When you are clear, it can be a tool to help you.

Maybe you are driven to prove that naysayer in your life wrong. Maybe you are trying to prove it to yourself or wish to silence that little voice in your head. Perfect. You are reading the right book at the right time.

Often, dreams seem so far off that we never truly commit to setting out on the journey. I get it. You'll hear how I started and stopped after a huge benchmark and why. I am writing this book to help you. To give you a simple, practical plan to help you get what you want or even become the person you want to be.

When I was eight years old, I dreamed of making people laugh. I soon realized I was not funny at all. I was told I shouldn't

even try. I was warned there are many things you can learn, but how to be funny ain't one of them. When I was twenty-six years old, I resurrected that dream. Nine years later, I had an audience of two thousand people laughing. Growing up, no one ever told me I'd be able to do that someday. But I did. That shy, quiet, naïve kid got to feel a moment he never thought possible. If I died tomorrow, it would be okay. I'm writing this book to wake up the little—or not so little—dreamer inside of you.

What if you are closer to your dream than you thought? What if tomorrow you were one step closer? What if you were just seventeen minutes from your next big breakthrough?

17 YOUR SEVENTEEN-MINUTE MISSION

▶ If being seventeen minutes away from your next big breakthrough sounds good, sit up a little straighter and keep reading.

▶ Where do you need sawgrass experience?

▶ Did you get clear on your why? This will be critical to get you through the plateaus on your journey.

▶ Create a list of sawgrass experiences you'll need to accomplish your dream and keep adding to it as new ideas come to you.

▶ Start a habit of action. Breakthroughs lay not in the new insight gained by reading but in the action that follows. Now is a chance to start the habit that will take you where you want to go.

CHAPTER 3:

WHAT WOULD YOU SAY TO YOU?

WHEN WE WERE kids, dreams flowed like rivers. We imagined what could be, what we could do, for hours. We didn't ask ourselves if we can. We just dreamed. That's what makes it a dream. Nothing is held back. There are no limitations or boundaries. We dream big. We didn't even know how to dream small. Why would we?

Then some well-meaning adults we trusted came along and taught us about reality. They told us what was actually possible. Maybe you heard, "That's not for us." Maybe, like me, you heard that success or wealth is for other people.

THEY TRAINED THE DREAM RIGHT OUT OF US.

We learn limitations, and like fleas in a covered jar, we believed them. God bless those kids who didn't listen or had parents who did not believe in limitations.

Look, I get it. Our well-meaning parents were trying to stop us from making fools of ourselves. They wanted us to save face. But I believe they should have told us, "Go for it!" They could have added, "You'll have to work harder than most people and will fall on your face more than most people, but I love you no matter what. I'll help you get up when you fall."

This book is about training the dream back into you. I want to give you a plan to be the person you need to become to own your dream. I know you're not reading this book to read a book. You are diving in to get the breakthroughs you are seeking to make your dream a reality.

Quick exercise: If you could go back and talk to eight-year-old you, what would you tell you? Take this seriously. Do you remember what you dreamed of back then? What you worried about? What you thought? In your mind, have a conversation with (or maybe write a letter to) the eight-year-old you.

Go ahead. Put this down for a second. Picture yourself sitting down with your eight-year-old self on two small wooden preschool chairs. You may tear up. It's OK if you do. Sometimes crying releases pains of your past and gives you bigger wings.

I did this myself, and it was fascinating. I listened to my own insecurities. How Mom dressed me in a bright red corduroy Sherlock Homes type coat and hat and how the other kids used to make fun of me and call me, "Darren, Darren, the Red Baron." I remembered working so hard with my dad making a pinewood derby racer in Scouts and how we came in last. It hurt losing. I felt like I disappointed Dad. He loved me anyway, yet I still felt like I let him down.

In my conversation with the young me, I would tell him, *"You are not going to be great at competitions for a long time, but don't give up because someday you will be a champion. I know you dream of being in movies, but you are going to become something even better."* I'd tell young me that you'll become who you need to become because of your failures and how you react to them. I'd make sure he understood that failures are a crucial part of success. I'd tell him that someday he would fail at a business, and because of that failure, he would inspire people around the world. I would ask, "What do you think of that?"

I can hear young me say, "You're really weird." I crack up just thinking about it. I'd do it anyway to make sure he knows failure is critical to success. I would have planted a seed that can grow and serve him.

So, what would *you* say to the eight-year-old you? What do you think the young you would say back to you? Try it! Listen! Feel! It can be helpful and enlightening.

Here's another exercise that can make this even better. What do you think the eighty-eight-year-old you would say to you, right now? Picture yourself sitting down in two wooden rocking chairs with the eighty-eight year-old you.

I thought that one through too. I could hear the wise-ass, eighty-eight-year-old me say, "Great advice you had for the kid. Ha-ha. Very encouraging. Maybe you should take that advice now yourself!"

That cracks me up. The truth often does.

I can hear him say to me, "The decisions you make now affect me, you know. The better decisions you make now will help me. But, more importantly, don't have any regrets. I don't want to sit on my rocking chair wishing I tried something. No regrets!

I can be much happier living without regrets. Just like you'd tell the kid, failures are part of getting the breakthroughs you need."

Wow. What a wake-up call. I know the eighty-eight-year-old me would call me out on taking a dose of my own medicine.

You and I only have today. Going backward can help us understand. Thinking forward can give us a sense of perspective and urgency. This is your dream and your life.

What would your eighty-eight-year-old self tell you today?

Remember this, your kids and grandkids are watching you. They are better at seeing what you do than hearing what you say. Think about that for a moment. If you won't do things for yourself, do it for them. Your actions are teaching them good or bad. The only question is, what are you teaching them?

This book is designed to train you to dream again. Dream big without limitations, then take a step every day. You are creating him or her by what you decide and act on today. Then listen to the eighty-eight-year-old you.

YOUR SEVENTEEN-MINUTE MISSION

▶ What would you tell the eight-year-old you?

▶ What did you worry about back then?

▶ What do you worry about now?

▶ What would the 88-year-old you tell you now?

▶ Today is all we have.

CHAPTER 4:

YOU ARE THE CEO OF YOUR DREAM

AFTER COLLEGE, I achieved my goal of opening a sub shop. In fact, in my head, that was just the first of many shops. I thought I'd become a millionaire for sure.

When revenue was light at the sub shop, I had to get a job to pay the employees and not default on my business loan. Between running the store and my second job, I worked from 9:00 a.m. to 1:00 a.m. almost seven days a week. I ended up having to sell the store at a loss. I was mad. It wasn't fair. I had bought into a successful franchise. I was mad at the franchise for allowing another one to open so close to mine. I was mad at the landlord. I was mad at God.

Years later, I was listening to a story from an amazing speaker, Jim Rohn. He told a story about how his mentor asked him to create a list of why he was not successful. He looked at Jim's list and said, "One problem with this list, Jim. Your name ain't on it." It hit me hard. I blamed everyone for my business failure, yet:

- I chose the franchise.

- I hired a lawyer and then ignored his advice.

- I chose the location.

- I chose not to follow the proven franchise success system because I was right out of business school and thought I knew better.

In a word, it was ego. It was one of the greatest lessons of my life. I was responsible.

And, yes, there are factors outside your control; there always will be. You are still responsible.

You are the CEO of your dream. Is that scary? Is that an eye-opener? Think about it. You can delegate, hire consultants, and have mentors, but you are still 100 percent responsible. Yes, 100 percent. It's your dream, not your parents', not your kids', not your friends'. It's yours. Own it!

Think about it. Dreams are *yours*. The desire is in your heart and no one else's. Yours!

Are we clear yet? Until you take ownership, nothing else matters. You determine the end goal. You decide the path you start on, and you choose when you change direction.

You might be like me. At times, I've been a horrible CEO of my dream. More often than I care to admit. I've also been an awful employee to myself. I didn't do the work I committed to, and I also didn't call myself out for not doing it. Doesn't that sound like colossal failure? Yep, and if you are not careful, victimhood soon follows, and it's time to phone the head of HR and plan a massive pity party. Whoop, whoop, boo-hoo—woe is me.

You can get opinions from others, but please make sure those opinions are from qualified people. Would a good CEO hire consultants in an area where they had zero experience? Would they look for only free advice or free articles they find on the internet by some blogger they never heard of? No. No. No. They would get advice from people who know what it takes in that area.

If you needed to hire someone to help you in a specific area, would you find just anyone willing to help at a low price? If you are hiring someone, don't ask your friend who has never hired someone for advice. Well-meaning, unqualified people will lead you in the wrong direction. Even if their heart is in the right place, only experienced people can guide from experience. The only thing worse than putting in a little effort is putting in lots of effort in the wrong direction. Doesn't that make sense?

Sometimes we get jealous of our bosses when we have jobs and clearly see they should have done things differently. I have. We think that policy isn't fair. In our head, we shout, "Why would they change the commission structure? That's stupid. Now, we'll make them rich, so they get a bonus." When you work for someone else, it can be easy to complain. You can focus on bitching about it or focus on making strides in a better direction. You are the CEO of your life too. Maybe it is the nudge you need to take control back and recalculate at a deeper level.

What are you *really* trying to accomplish?

When you are the CEO, you can't complain because you are the boss.

If you have people who are trying to help but aren't helping, fire them. Even if they used to help, if they aren't now, they need to lose their position of helper in your dream. That may be difficult, but it reveals a truth we need to embrace.

DREAMS ARE NOT CONVENIENT.

Being the boss isn't easy. No dream has ever been accomplished on a straight path. Adjustments will always be required along the way. Reevaluation is necessary.

Do you know what's *not* necessary? To know exactly how things will happen. I doubt any big dream was accomplished by perfect execution. Every worthwhile journey has its own unique "Houston, we have a problem" moment.

Many perfectionists will never fully achieve their dream. Why? Because they are perfectionists. We need to strive forward before everything is perfect. As we move forward, we will get more intel, and we can course-correct. In my career as a keynote speaker, I've learned great speeches aren't written. They are rewritten. And you can't edit what you don't create. It's the same for any worthwhile mission. You can't course-correct without some intel from your own experience.

There are some other things you can't do. You can't delegate your dream. You can't love living someone else's dream. You can't keep making excuses about your own. A good CEO doesn't allow excuses. You don't have to know the whole journey upfront. You have to start while not knowing. If you are looking for excuses, you'll find them. If you are looking for your top priority to focus on today, you'll find that too.

Be honest with yourself. What are you seeking?

If you aren't quite sure where to start, good news: I've got the answer. It begins with a commitment and owning the fact that you are the CEO of your dream. The second step is getting qualified advice on the best habits to create a proven process to start following. It does not mean it will be easy or simple. It also doesn't mean you may not get bad advice from time to time. Just keep doing your due diligence. Realize it's all part of the journey to achieving your dream. You might even consider it a test to see if you are serious or not. Are you?

In 1992, I decided I was going to try standup comedy, just once. Thanks to pumping myself with motivational tapes, I knew to get advice from someone successful at it. I went to a headliner come-dian after a show. I worked up the courage to ask, "Hi, my name is Darren. I want to try standup; what do I need to do?" He told me to get a specific book. Ah, direction. A path to start down. Perfect.

Let me ask: Who is more important in the process of accom-plishing a dream, the student or the teacher? Think about it before you read the following sentence. There are many great teachers out there, but I say the student is much more impor-tant. What's critically important is you, as the student, finding the right teacher, for you, as the student. If the teacher isn't helping you, choose another. Remember, you are the CEO. By the way, I'm going to beat this idea into you because it's essen-tial to you achieving your dream.

Not every mentor is the right mentor. Throughout my journey, I've had many mentors. Each taught me something different while confirming some common essentials. As a trainer of professional speakers, I've had many students come through our world-class workshops. Some become successful, and others do not. The course is solid, but it's what the student does with it that truly causes the transformation. You bring you to everything you do. When you force yourself to get breakthroughs, you transform who you are. Find the right mentors and teachers. Be a sponge. If it truly is a dream that you are committed to, there may be many lessons and allies you need to attract along the way to your dream.

Remember, you bring you to a course. You bring you to a relationship. You bring you to a coach. When I first started working with my coach, my insecurities and ego were in the way. I had to change who I was to be a better student. I learned an invaluable lesson: If you are not coachable, there is no cure.

Are you ready to rehire yourself as CEO? Are you prepared to recommit? Remind yourself each morning. Say it out loud and own it. "I am the CEO of my dream." Okay, what will you do today?

17 YOUR SEVENTEEN-MINUTE MISSION

▶ Ask yourself, again, where do you need sawgrass experience?

▶ Do you understand that you are the CEO of your dream?

▶ Who on your team do you need to fire?

▶ Who do you need to hire? (Even if it is a qualified friend you aren't paying. Note the word "qualified.")

▶ Want a daily dose of inspiration? Go to: 365InspirationalQuotes.com.

CHAPTER 5

TEDDY SAID IT BEST

TEDDY SAID IT best. Who's Teddy? We'll get to that.

First, let's talk about you. One of the critical steps you need to take toward your dream is your next one. You got this book, which is the first step for you. (Congratulations.)

As you walk forward on your journey, at some point, an essential move will be stepping into the public eye. There is much you can do behind the curtain, but there will be a time when others discover your dream. My goal now is to prepare you for that moment.

When you put yourself out there, whether online or to a small group of friends over dinner, be aware and prepare yourself for potential naysayers. Let me give you an example that happened recently:

My marketing mentor, Ford Saeks, and I delivered our "Get Paid to Speak" free training. Our goal is to help people, whether they choose to join our program or not. The content is solid, but you can't teach everything about the business in fifty-nine minutes. There is no way. We can't even do that in a two-day workshop because business, social media, and marketing are always changing.

We delivered the training, and it went well. We had fun, gave rock-solid insights, and as a result, got many new members to join us to learn more. Cool. We allow people who could not attend live forty-eight hours to watch the replays at their convenience. We've learned through experience that if they don't watch it within those forty-eight hours, they won't watch it at all. It's what experience (the sawgrass) and the numbers tell us.

As I'm a fan of constant improvement, we send a follow-up email a day later and ask for feedback. Be careful what you ask for. Though I won't mention any names, here is part of one email that came in:

Subject: Re: Quick help...I'm looking for feedback.

Where was the beef?

It was all talky talk bullWaste of time.

There is more real info for free than anything you could credibly sell me.

SameYour personal story. Which could be fabricated. How great is this program. Blah; Blah, Blah!

Find another sucker.

Only the internet seperates you from a street corner snake oil salesmen.

I wonder if this person yells at TV commercials instead of paying for Netflix?

Did I mention it was *free*? Did I mention many people loved it so much they invested in learning more? When you put yourself out there, you'll find, Dorothy, that you're not in Kansas anymore. You'll quickly realize that some people aren't quite as nice as your close, inspired friends.

Their words may be negative and critical, but maybe there's a nugget of truth in there? Are you confident enough to ask yourself? Remember, it's the experience. It's touching the sawgrass that makes the difference. If you process this properly and don't take it personally, it can serve you on your journey. Don't ever stop because of that; just learn, regroup, and keep going. Remember when we said adjustments would happen along the way?

Even if they are correct, it is only one moment in time that they are talking about. Do not let that one moment define you. It's not just the experience of giving it and living it, but how you react *after* it. How do you take that? Reformulate and improve the presentation.

Here's another email I received. This guy was mad because I only let him watch the free replays for forty-eight hours. The email said:

Sorry, since I only had 24-48 hours to view the **Get Paid to Speak** video, and the next days were inconvenient, I didn't view it - so no feedback. I was hoping the video would be available longer to view at MY convenience not YOURS.

Suggestion, when signing up to attend or view the video later, please state EXACTLY in the registration who long one has to view (either "Can view video until mm/dd/yyyy"). If I'd known I only would have so short a time to view it, I'd never has registered.

Did I mention it was *free*? Yes, I could give more time, but I know that deadlines get people to move. Sometimes, there is a nugget of truth in criticisms that we can learn from. This was not that situation. He could have easily signed up again for another forty-eight hours, but honestly, I'm not going to tell him that. Why? I don't want his business. If he's that upset and demanding about something free, imagine how he would be if he were paying for our courses. I fire members, especially those who are disrespectful to my staff. I don't want any complainers around me. Not every dollar is a good one.

You have probably heard the quote from George Bernard Shaw, from his drama *Man and Superman*: "Those who can, do; those who can't, teach."

Don't you dare let a critic stop you! It's just information. What's important is how we process that information. But some people think that experience defines them. I love getting the experience, and then teaching from it. I believe that helps me be a better teacher. In all honesty, it took me a long time not to take it personally. What I've learned is when you can focus down the road, it makes today's bumps smaller.

THOSE WHO CAN'T, CRITIQUE. You and I can't give the critic too much power. Here is my reply to that quote: "Those who can't, critique."

Toastmasters are clubs for people who want to improve their public speaking. They have an annual contest, which began in 1938, called the World Championship of Public Speaking. You can find my speech by doing a YouTube search for "Darren LaCroix winning speech."

When I was running around from club to club, a man pulled me aside after the meeting. He asked if I'd ever heard of Teddy Roosevelt's 1910 speech, "Man in the Arena."

I had not. So, I researched it. Oh my gosh, I loved it. It spoke to me. It still speaks to me. If you haven't heard it, check this out. If you have, I'll ask you to reread it and see how it applies to your dream at this time. Teddy said it best:

> *It is not the critic who counts; not the man who points out how the strong man stumbles or where the doer of deeds could have done them better. The credit belongs to the man who is actually in the arena, whose face is marred by dust and sweat and blood; who strives valiantly; who errs, who comes short again and again, because there is no effort without error and shortcoming; but who does actually strive*

to do the deeds; who knows the great enthusiasms, the great devotions; who spends himself in a worthy cause; who at the best knows in the end the triumph of high achievement, and who at the worst, if he fails, at least fails while daring greatly, so that his place shall never be with those cold and timid souls who knew neither victory nor defeat.

What are you striving for? What's your arena?

Let me be crystal clear, especially to my fellow Toastmasters: When you put yourself out there for the world to see, someone will critique everything you do, whether you ask them for feedback or not. Nice, well-meaning people will stab you with a word or two and follow it up with, "I'm just trying to help." Well, that's one way to look at it.

Remember, you are the CEO of your dream. We have a common phrase where I come from in Boston. It's, "Shut up!" Add them to your list of people you will pleasantly prove wrong. Don't argue with them; that wasted energy could be better used more efficiently by taking the next steps. Eventually, they will catch on that they just fueled your fire. Some will even apologize. It's rare, but can happen.

Back in my comedy days, I took a class with a TV comedy writer from Hollywood, Stanley Ralph Ross. He had written many TV programs, including *Batman*, *The Monkees*, and *All In the Family*. He towered over me and was a big, brilliant teddy bear with a gruff voice. He was encouraging with a big dose of truth.

In the middle of one of our classes, he talked about this very subject. He looked right at me and, in a matter-of-fact tone, said, "People are going to tell you, 'You suck.'"

That was it. And it was powerful. It's part of the process, like victories and plateaus. Now, when people say something like that to me, I smile and say to myself, "There's another one Stan warned me about."

Sometimes, the naysayers will be friends and family. People who care for us. This can be more challenging and more likely to stop you or drain your hope. They may know you, but they may not know you on a mission. I had been that wimp who had easily been told about reality and was easily talked out of things. Let me give you a new perspective. Let naysayers be a test. A reminder to see if you are committed or not. What if they were just a test to see if you are serious? They are! When you keep going, or as I say, "Take the step after the ouch," you pass that test. You have two options as CEO: You can let them stop you or get you to dig in your heels a little deeper. You can use their comments as fuel to prove them wrong. One naysayer said to me, "You? No one will ever pay you a dollar to make people laugh." I had a porcelain comedy and tragedy mask on my wall. I wrapped up the first dollar I earned, rolled it up, and stuck it in the tragedy mask's mouth. It is still in my office today.

Having this mindset can prepare you for those inevitable naysayers. You can become unstoppable. Because of my lack of confidence growing up, I naively believed everyone knew more than me. Now, I know they know *differently* than me. Big difference. Have the confidence to look for a grain of truth, that may be a lesson that needs to be learned, but don't you dare let it stop you. It's easy to be the critic. It's more challenging to be the person in the arena.

Last word of caution on this subject. Don't be your own worst critic. That little voice in your head can be the most critical one of all. It can be persuasive. Why don't you fire your inner critic? You can because you are the CEO of your dream.

YOUR
SEVENTEEN-MINUTE
MISSION

▶ Yet again: Where do you need sawgrass experience?

▶ And again: Do you understand that you are the CEO of your dream?

▶ Will you listen to the critic or your own heart?

▶ Remember Stan's wisdom, "People will tell you, 'You suck!'"

CHAPTER 6

WHAT WILL IT FEEL LIKE?

WHAT WILL IT feel like when you achieve your dream? How about when you reach your benchmarks along the way? The pursuit of your dreams will produce feelings that go along with the accomplishments and setbacks experienced along the way.

Back in 2000, I was still living at home with my parents after a devastating business failure. Much of it was my fault. I had some important lessons to learn that were critical to my success today. I had sold my business at a loss. Which meant I still had a business loan to pay off and no business to do that with.

The other challenge was I was still paying off my college loans. Oh, and I had a crazy dream to become a professional speaker, all while I was living at home with Mom and Dad. My day job income was used to help pay off the loans, pay Mom and Dad rent, and pursue my dream. I worked as a telemarketer in a maze of cubicles. I felt like Chris Farley's motivational speaker character on Saturday Night Live, "I live in a van, down by the river!" (If you are too young to know it, check it out on YouTube.)

I was nearing the point of paying off both loans and had booked a big keynote speech in Bermuda. The flexibility of my day job allowed me to take a couple days off and deliver the speech, then come back to finish my hours for the week. During the convention in Bermuda, we had an afternoon to play. Some of my new friends from the conference invited me to rent scooters and tour the island.

As I scooted by the ocean's edge and smelled the saltwater, I found myself in heaven. It felt amazing. Looking over to my left, I could see crystal clear water. The tropical breeze cooled me off. Amazing! At that moment, a dream was born. I *had* to have this feeling again. I decided I needed to buy a motorcycle after I was debt-free.

I was now on a mission. The feeling inspired me. Finally, the moment came. I gave a speech in Florida for a network marketing company. I had my best back-of-the-room sales. (Remember CDs and DVDs? I'm so glad I don't need to lug or ship them anymore.) I sold $23,000 worth of my merchandise. It was a record-busting moment for me—I was thrilled. I had disciplined myself to pay off the two major loans before I could spoil myself with the motorcycle.

I finished paying off both loans. I bought my brand-new motorcycle in cash. No debt. The motorcycle was Darren-sized. As a short guy, when I straddled the bike, I wanted my feet to lay flat on the ground at stoplights. It was red and gray. It was mine. I loved it. As many guys do, I also bought the matching costume to complete the look.

After moving to Las Vegas in 2013, I loved riding it even more. Unlike living in New England, I could drive it most of the year. My favorite became cruising through beautiful Red Rock Canyon, only thirty minutes from my home. It was my little getaway. I started calling it my "product bike" because I bought it with profits from my educational tools. That was a feeling I'll never forget.

What will the feeling be like when you achieve your dream? Can you imagine it? Do you smile when you think about it? I hope so. Hold on to it. You'll need to reflect on that during the bumps and plateaus that may seem like they will never end. They will, but you have to keep going. Rejoice when break-throughs happen. Take the time to feel them.

YOUR SEVENTEEN-MINUTE MISSION

▶ As asked before, where do you need sawgrass experience?

▶ Yet again, do you understand that you are the CEO of your dream?

▶ Will you listen to the critic or your own heart?

▶ What will accomplishing the steps to your dream feel like?

▶ Remember to get a daily dose of inspiration. Go to: 365InspirationalQuotes.com

CHAPTER 7

BUT WAIT, WHAT ABOUT MY RESPONSIBILITIES?

WHAT IS BETWEEN where you are now and where you want to be? The distance may be shorter than you think. That's exciting.

But, I know, I know. You have responsibilities.

I can hear it now, "Oh, but I have a job. I have a house to clean. I have a mortgage. I have projects that I have to finish first. I gotta take care of my spouse, the kids. As soon as the kids…"

I get it. But guess what?

Dreams are not convenient.

There will never be a perfect time. Ever. Wouldn't you love to be much further along than you are today? What if you are letting that inner critic stop you with excuses? Let's face it: Dreams take courage. Do you want your kids and grandkids to have courage? Remember, they are watching what you do more than they're listening to the words you say. Inspire by example: you will fail, and they will see you fall. So, give them real-life examples close to home to teach them how to get up and keep moving forward with courage and conviction.

How can you possibly go for that dream when you have responsibilities? I'll show you an example from my life. Back when I was an emerging speaker, as I mentioned, I had a day job. I was a telemarketer at Bose Corporation as I paid off my debts. I was pursuing my dream at the same time. The local newspaper did an article about people who are juggling their dreams and their day jobs. The article was titled: "Juggling the Day and Dreams." I was one of the people they interviewed. The article's cover showed a picture of me acting in a local TV spot and another of me at my desk wearing my telemarketing headset. I say that to tell you that you're not alone in your challenges. People who are seriously committed find a way despite them. Will you?

"THE MIGHTY OAK IS JUST A NUT THAT HELD ITS GROUND."

–ANONYMOUS

I had many days where I thought, "What was I thinking?" There were days when I saw no progress. In fact, at times, it felt like I was going backward. I let that inner critic shout, and he made a lot of logical sense. (By the way, dreams are rarely rational.)

What kept me going on the bad days? If you were able to zoom in close on that picture in the newspaper, you'd see something on my pushpin board in front of where I sat. Strategically in front of me were a few motivational quotes. I stared at them as I made my calls every day.

In my head, I customized the second one by saying to myself, "If there is a voice inside you that says, 'You cannot make people laugh,' then make them laugh. That voice will be silenced."

What do you have in front of you, staring you in the face, reminding you to keep going? We all need it. That constant reminder to keep pressing on. If you have something that works for you already, cool. If not, how about making that something you do today? Maybe you have something in front of you that *used* to inspire you. If it no longer does, perhaps it's time for an upgrade. Get something that speaks to you *now*. Remember, you are the CEO, so you can decide to remodel a bit. Changing things in your surroundings for the better reminds you that you're growing and going somewhere.

"IF YOU HEAR A VOICE WITHIN YOU THAT SAYS, 'YOU CANNOT PAINT,' THEN, BY ALL MEANS, PAINT, AND THAT VOICE WILL BE SILENCED."
—VINCENT VAN GOGH

Making people laugh on stage was a huge dream, but I made sure I followed my dream while taking care of my responsibilities. For example, though I got a sweet deal on rent from Mom and Dad, I still paid it. At the same time, I slowly paid down my loans.

I was also pursuing my dream, but trust me, there were days I would look at that quote and think, "Only through you, God. How am I going to keep going?" You may be thinking, "Can I do this?" I get it because I asked the same question. But I did it, and you can too.

Are you adding too much drama to your dream? I know I did. I made my challenges worse in my head. Consider this, "Dreams can be a sheep in wolf's clothing."

Yes, reread it. It's the opposite of the cliché. Don't let your inner critic fool you. Don't make the roadblocks bigger in your head. Sometimes the thoughts about our roadblocks are bigger than the roadblocks themselves. The irony is we focus on the negative thoughts instead of focusing on how to get around, through, or over them. Catch yourself and make the necessary changes.

Let's continue. Maybe it's shorter than you think. We all have responsibilities.

▶ Take inventory of your environment. What can you put right in front of you to remind you to press on?

▶ Do you remember that you are the CEO of your dream?

▶ Do you listen to the critic or more often to your own heart?

▶ What will achieving your dream feel like?

▶ What if you can still take care of your responsibilities *and* go for it?

CHAPTER 8

WHAT'S YOUR NINEVEH?

WAS DELIVERING A keynote speech in Vancouver, Canada, for a group of speakers. I had told my story of how I went from chump to champ. I covered the critical habits, mentors, and breakthroughs I had to win the World Championship of Public Speaking. There was extra time, and I love opening up for questions. A bold young buck raised his hand and asked, "I loved your story, but what's the dream you are working on now?" Great question. For my friends who are motivational speakers, this may sting a bit, but what are *you* striving for now? Are you living your talk? (Walking sounds too boring and cliché to me.) How dare I not move toward my next dream?

Nineveh was a city in the Middle East in biblical times. If you don't know the story, God wanted Jonah to go and preach there. Nineveh was Jonah's destiny.

What is yours?

You have a destiny, a calling, a dream. What is it? What is it that compels you down deep? What do you feel you are supposed to accomplish? What's that deep-seated desire that pops up on occasion? It makes you smile for a moment, but then you are distracted by real life. What is that dream that quietly haunts you?

So, how did I answer that bold young man? What's mine *now*? Well, it came to life with a simple question in a restaurant booth. It was a mastermind meeting at BJ's Brewhouse. Several keynote speakers, including Marilyn Sherman and Mike Rayburn, were getting together to help each other out. Mike was a rock star in the National Speakers Association and had just moved to town. So, as we sat in this circular booth, he posed a deep question. He asked, "What is your crazy, big, ridiculous dream?"

I remember I went last. I sheepishly, and in a wishy-washy manner, spoke up, "Well, you know, I kind of always loved true-life movies. And I remember when the movie *Rudy* came out in 1993. I had started comedy in 1992. That story moved me and kept me going. I've always been drawn to true-life inspirational stories. I had to see every one of them. I got to meet the real Rudy. He told me how he had his movie made. And I thought, 'Well, what if I make a movie about my story? I've been telling my story from the stage for years. But who am I to have a movie made about my life?'"

Those words, "But who am I to have a movie made about my life," immediately triggered something in Mike. He had been listening intently to my insecurely delivered answer and, without warning, jumped up, leaned in so he was just inches from my face, stuck his index finger out, and with mentor-like conviction, said, "Who are you not to?"

It felt like he reached inside me, pulled up my dream front and center, and made it real. I was not the same after that moment.

If you took the time to answer that question sincerely, how would you reply? Who are you not to live out the dream God put in your heart? Who are you to not respond to the inspiration that comes from somewhere deep? Who are you not to?

My own "lack" thinking kept my dream buried. When I said it out loud and got approval from a man I respected—boom. It came to life.

I got excited. Real excited. I was on a mission. I decided to start by heading off to Hollywood to find a writer like Rudy had for his movie. I had to start somewhere. I delivered a training in LA, and in the room, unbeknownst to me, was an actor-turned-producer. I asked her for advice on finding a writer, and she said, "I just saw you speak; you need to write the screenplay yourself." What? I didn't know how to do that. She went on to tell me she and her husband make movies for the Hallmark channel, and she reads scripts all day long. She said the biggest problem she sees is structure. She encouraged me to get a book by Syd Field. Ironically, it instantly felt like I went back to 1992 in the comedy club, where I was told my first step was to get the book. That made me smile.

I learned two critical insights I hope will help you:

#1. WHEN PURSUING A DREAM THAT IS NOT IN YOUR WHEELHOUSE, LISTEN TO PEOPLE WITH REAL-LIFE EXPERIENCES. A woman who was in the thick of Hollywood experience suggested a book. I didn't flinch. Done. I couldn't buy the book soon enough.

I had learned that lesson from my previous crazy dream's beginning. The best thing I did was get direction from people who were in the arena. When a book was recommended to me by a headliner comedian, I immediately went out and bought it. We need to start our trajectory in a proven direction. You don't need to get *a* book; you need to get the *right* book or take the right course. Who can tell you which one is the right one?

#2. BE WILLING TO TAKE THE UNEXPECTED DETOUR. If people who are where you want to be suggest a slightly different path, take it. After many pursuits, Rudy found a writer. I followed that idea, but when Ms. Producer said I need to write it myself instead of finding a writer, I did—well, after a big, nervous gulp. It was not my plan, but it is now.

A couple of months later, Patricia Fripp called. She was attending a screenwriter's summit and invited me to join her. I asked who was teaching, and she mentioned several names, including her friend Michael Hauge. I had never heard of any of them, including Michael Hauge. Then, she said, "Oh, there is one more. I think his name is Syd Field?" What? The guy who wrote the book that I'm reading? Yep. I took that as a huge God wink, knew I was on the right path, and immediately registered.

It was December 9, 2012. At the Screenwriters' Summit, I learned a Hollywood script needs to be in the correct format. I had no idea. I invested in the software. I took classes. I got mentors. I read more books. I did the exercises.

Have you noticed that sometimes we read the book but don't do the exercises that are in the book? We feel like we need to get to the next chapter. No. Stop and do the exercises. Why? Because it's that sawgrass experience that we need. Yes, we need to input the data. But it's going through the exercise that transforms who we are and moves us closer to our dream. We need that experience touching the sawgrass.

I started on my screenwriting journey. Writing a single story in 100 percent dialogue was a different animal. It was challenging. I decided to write once a week. I struggled. I learned another valuable lesson: Don't work on your dream once per week. You lose momentum. In this book, you are tapping into my experience chasing two crazy dreams. You'll get some "do this" and some "don't do this." Working once a week on your dream is a "don't do this."

I was told if you are going to write a screenplay, you should study them. Duh. When I was working on my international contest speech, I looked at ten years of contest videos. Back then, there were nine contestants each year, so I studied ninety world-class speeches. Think about that. I was intently trying to figure out the tiny difference between the person who came in first and the person who came in second. My coach could have told me what the difference was (telling me about the sawgrass), or I could intently dive in and study until I got it at a deep level myself (by actually touching the sawgrass). There is a huge difference. With this dream, I was told to study screenplays, so I tracked down the scripts to my favorite movies similar to the one I wanted to write. I found the scripts to *Rudy, The Rookie, Miracle, The Blind Side,* and *Soul Surfer.*

You may have heard about the ten-million-dollar check Jim Carrey wrote himself for "acting services rendered." He kept it in his wallet to help him stay focused on his dream. That was another important "do this" lesson I learned from chasing my first dream. I needed a constant reminder. The first time, motivational quotes were in the corporate beige pushpin board at my day job desk. This time, I needed a symbol of a completed successful feature film. What would that be? A movie poster. I looked at the movie posters for *Rudy* and *The Rookie* with Dennis Quaid and hired a designer to make a poster for my future movie. I even added quotes and stars that I could picture being in the film. I had it blown up and put in my office. I also made it my phone's home-screen image.

That poster is the new motivational image I keep in front of me. What's your constant reminder?

I've also kept myself motivated by staying focused on my why. Remember in an earlier chapter when I asked you to go deeper into your why? You may be wondering about my deeper why. Why this movie?

I grew up in New England and celebrated the holidays with the Polish side of our family. The smells of pierogi and kielbasa filled Grandma's house. The sight of chocolate roll and Mom's chocolate cream pie could make you drool. When all my cousins were together at Grandma's house, they needed to add the standard card table, affectionately called the "kid's table." It wobbled a bit. What always made me smile was the joy and laughter in the air. My twin aunts had harmonious, infectious laughter. My cousins and my brother always had the family laughing. I was just in awe of their abilities to make people laugh.

Making people laugh was *not* in my skill set. Not even close. I was the shy naïve kid sitting back and enjoying the show. One time, when I was eight years old, I got so caught up in the moment, I stood up and shouted out a line. I expected laughs, but instead, it instantly hushed my family. Yikes. I was embarrassed. I slid down in my little chair and told myself, "I will never ever try to be funny again." I stuck to that. I pursued my love of business. I was an entrepreneur.

Fast forward to 1992. After my devastating business failure, I was listening to a motivational tape of Brian Tracy. He asked, "What would you dare to dream if you knew you wouldn't fail?" That question tapped directly into that little eight-year-old dreamer inside me. The one who was told, "That's not for you." And, "You're just not funny." Now twenty-three years old, that question brought my dream back to life.

I've always been enamored with true-life movies about someone accomplishing something no one thought was possible. I have to get this movie made to inspire the eight-year-old dreamer in you and all the people who were told, "No, you can't." People who were lied to by well-meaning naysayers. I got to stand on a stage and inspire two thousand people while making them laugh. Now, I feel like it is my responsibility to wake up the little dreamer in other people like you, with the same mission questions.

17 YOUR SEVENTEEN-MINUTE MISSION

▶ Will you listen intently to people with real-life experience?

▶ Are you ready and willing to take unexpected detours?

▶ Will you listen to the critic or your own heart?

▶ What's your Nineveh? What is that whisper of a dream that you keep thinking about?

CHAPTER 9

THE WHALE

O N July 15, 2019, I presented Mike Rayburn, the guy who slammed his hands down and said, "Who are you not to?" a copy of that script. That was a cool moment. The feeling was indescribable. I hope you've had a feeling like that and, more importantly, can share it again soon with someone who encouraged you to reach your dream.

Okay, the script was done. Now, I needed to sell it to Hollywood. Deep breath. "How am I going to do that?" I honestly didn't know. I have since learned that there are over 30,000 scripts registered with the writer's guild each year. Only a handful of them reaches the big screen. Gulp. Well, Mike did ask me what my big crazy dream was back at that restaurant years ago.

I reached out to a mentor, Jim, who had his book turned into a Universal Studios film. Remember to ask people who have been in the arena, not your well-meaning friends. Jim told me that I needed to get the script in the hands of one hundred people in Hollywood to have five good conversations. Yes, a number. Did I mention I am a numbers geek? I started a spreadsheet to track my way to one hundred conversations. How hard could that be? Um, we'll get back to that.

One of the books also suggested looking up antecedents, movies similar to mine, to learn their box office numbers. You can then share those when pitching producers and movie companies. I looked up movies like *Rudy*, *The Rookie*, *Miracle*, *The Blind Side*, and *Soul Surfer*. I looked them up on BoxOfficeMojo.com. I also researched the movie companies, producers, and directors for these films on IMDB.com. It was exciting. But, though some of this may have become helpful, it was a distraction from my main focus. I needed to be making calls and getting the scripts in the hands of anyone I could. The research was good, but the actual reaching out is more important. If you are anything like me, we can sometimes confuse being busy with making real progress. Sometimes it is because of self-doubt.

BEWARE OF DISTRACTIONS DISGUISED AS OPPORTUNITIES.

Get clear on what people in the arena tell you is most important. I'll always remember one brilliant quote Mike Rayburn said: "Beware of distractions disguised as opportunities."

In the Bible story of Jonah, God sent Jonah to Nineveh, and he ran the other way. He went to Joppa, jumped on a ship, got thrown overboard, and swallowed by a big fish. I don't know too many fish that are big enough to swallow a man, so I'll call it a whale. He was in the belly of the whale for three days before he finally realized what he needed to do. He repented and asked for God's help. Once he did, the whale spit him out on a beach. Then he finally did what he was supposed to do by going to Nineveh.

Your dream was put on *your* heart, no one else's. Here is my big question for you: Have you been swallowed by the whale of self-doubt?

Seriously, have you been swallowed by the whale of self-doubt? If you feel like you have, I get it. I was all excited about selling the script, and it felt courageous because I had no idea what I was doing. I had no big insider contacts. I doubted and made excuses.

Our responsibilities and life incidents can also add to our doubt. We have a life, and we have priorities. Our dreams still need a little bit of attention to stay alive. I've got a strategy to help you with that. I wished I'd used it back in 2019. I wrote this book to help you avoid the mistake I made.

HAVE YOU BEEN SWALLOWED BY THE WHALE OF SELF-DOUBT?

Here is a bit of transparency from my world back then: I stopped knowing what was going on in my business. I had put my head in the sand. I was still working hard, but I had this dream that was taking most of my attention. I was so excited about my dream that I didn't pay enough attention to my business numbers. My business credit debt was $58,126.66. I was paying $1,431.82 a month in interest on that debt. I went through all of my savings.

On the upside, I quickly learned that I could buy a box of mac and cheese for one dollar and split it into two meals. I had to sell the motorcycle I loved so much to pay my mortgage one month.

I started to doubt myself again. So, if you've doubted yourself, welcome to the club! We all have, and you're not alone.

All of this doesn't mean you should stop. You need to take care of responsibilities *and* continue pursuing your dream.

The strategy you are about to get could have helped me through this. My doubt got me to lose myself in *Forensic Files* and *Law & Order* binge-watching. I love those shows. But, feeling depressed as I tried to keep my business from collapsing, I would sit on the couch watching them, feeling sorry for myself. I spiraled down. I prayed but found I had more doubt than faith.

I don't say all of this to get you to feel bad for me. It was my fault. I let it happen. I am responsible.

I'm telling you because I don't want you to do the same thing. If I had put some effort in, even a little, I could have been making progress and been building my belief. Take care of your responsibilities while you keep building your belief. One more episode of a drama-filled crime show did not help me. Don't be fooled. It can be a drama-filled distraction that just leads to another episode. Don't do this. Focus on your mission.

▶ Where do you need sawgrass experience?

▶ Do you understand that you are the CEO of your dream?

▶ Will you listen to the critic or your own heart?

▶ What will achieving your dream feel like?

▶ What if you can still take care of your responsibilities *and* go for it?

▶ What's your Nineveh? What is that whisper of a dream that you keep thinking about?

▶ What can you do to get out of the whale of self-doubt?

▶ Are you stopping you? If you are, then you can stop stopping you.

CHAPTER 10

THE UNDERDOG EFFECT

ACK IN MY early comedy days, I was taking to heart what my mentors had told me. I did whatever they said, even when it was uncomfortable. When they said jump, I didn't just say, "How high?" I also said, "How often?" I was open, eager, and, you might say, a sponge. Unlike my early days owning a franchise when I thought I knew better, I now knew that I didn't know. That is invaluable, especially when you are going into uncharted territory.

I learned any day I didn't go on stage was a day that I didn't grow. The challenge was that there were only so many open-mic nights in the Boston area. Most of them were horrible settings. I'm talking in a bar, at a bowling alley, standing on a milk crate. Did I mention you would have to compete with the TV at the bar? Not ideal, but you had to earn your way from the horrible settings to the real shows in the real comedy clubs.

There were times when, if I couldn't go on stage in Boston, I'd drive two and a half hours to Portland, Maine, to go on stage for five minutes and drive back and go to my day job early the next morning. It may sound crazy, but that's what I thought I needed to do. So, I did. My high school buddies told me that was stupid. Be careful who you listen to.

About a year and a half into my comedy career, I remember an open-mic night at the Comedy Connection in downtown Boston. I had just come off stage, getting a few small laughs in my five-minute set. I thought, "Tough crowd." I sat with my mentor, Vinnie. We watched a new comic go up on stage for the first time. He crushed it. The new guy had non-stop laughs. Good for him, but what am I doing wrong?

I was disgusted. I had been busting my butt for over a year and making little progress, and it was his first night. I turned to Vinnie and asked, "How do you know who is going to make it?" He matter-of-factly said, "That's easy; whoever keeps going." We can't compare our journey to anyone else's. Period.

Then he took a drag of his cigarette and said, "You've been taking that stage time thing to heart. I like that." Then he said, "I'm a headline comedian. I play all over New England at the best clubs. I'm going to give you five minutes of stage time wherever I play." What? Are you kidding? Then he leaned in and got right in my face and said, "But if you ever turn down stage time, I'll never help you again." What just happened? How did that happen?

I believe when you are all-in, people notice. They want to help the humble person striving and willing to make mistakes and get up and keep going. When you are humble and all-in, people of influence come alongside you. Whether you think it is God or the universe, something happens. There is a multiplying effect to your efforts. It is the same thing I noticed in high school football. I was completely committed, fully focused—all-in—and eventually, my skills developed, and the coaches noticed. I call it the "underdog effect." People root for the underdog because their odds are against them. People want to help people who are striving for the impossible. It works.

We know about intelligence quotient (IQ), emotional intelligence or quotient (EQ), and artificial intelligence (AI). I'd like to introduce you to a different concept, one that I've experienced. I believe it is an underlying factor to all underdogs who achieve the seemingly impossible. I call it AII, "all-in intelligence."

I think when you have the all-in mindset, people are compelled to come alongside you and help. Your dedication inspires people who want to help. It makes you stand out to mentors and people of influence as well. The surge builds, and you get noticed. Why? Because it's so rare. People will go from cheering you on to asking, "How can I help?"

It's one thing to be the person in the arena. You also want to turn the naysayers into believers. Show them. Ever see a mom determined to clean up a disaster in the house? She yells at the kids who caused it to help. They won't. She says, "Fine, but you can't leave the room until it's clean." They say, "Fine," and sit there. She indignantly grabs the vacuum and starts alone. No one moves. But the wake of inspiration created by Mom doing what needs to be done slowly flows through the room. One kid gets up and says, "I'll pick up the toys, but I'm not dusting." Mom doesn't flinch. She keeps at it. Soon, every kid is pitching in because Mom is all-in.

WHEN YOUR WHY RUNS DEEP, YOUR WAKE FLOWS WIDE.

When you have the resolve and make that commitment, something magical happens. I can't explain why, but I bet you have witnessed it. I'm suggesting you use this universal underdog effect in your favor. Become that person on a mission that people suddenly want to come alongside and help. Be all-in—they'll notice.

A few years ago, fellow World Champion of Public Speaking, Craig Valentine and I led a two-day workshop in Baltimore called "Get Coached to Speak." At this event, VIPs get personal two-on-one coaching from Craig and me. That is what they invested in. We have so much fun together while transforming the VIPs together. Before the event, Craig banged up his knee coaching basketball for his son. Yikes for him, and yikes for our students as he had to have emergency surgery. What would we do?

We did not have much time. We looked to our students, who were out coaching speakers and doing it at a world-class level. It was unanimous; we both agreed Mike Davis was getting the call. He was elated that we chose him and a bit nervous. We flew him out to the event, and he delivered. He had taken all of our courses, been to all of our events, making it happen for himself. We noticed. When you are all-in, people will notice. We did. That is why Mike got the call. Since then, Mike has become an amazing emcee at our events, hosting our online coaching calls and coaches alongside us as equal colleagues. We noticed.

When I asked Mike about this story and how he came to be all-in, he told me something that surprised me. Remember the story of my mentor at the beginning of this chapter? It is also a story I told from the stage for years. Well, Mike Davis heard that story when I met him in 2002. He said whenever he was going to turn down stage time (a.k.a., minutes), he heard my mentor's voice in his head: "If you ever turn down stage time, I'll never help you again." That story helped Mike be all-in. Because he was all-in, he got breakthroughs he would not have obtained otherwise. I sincerely hope it helps you too.

On January 1, my buddy Mark Kamp and some of his friends

did an all-in polar plunge. Even though we live in Las Vegas, the water is cold on January 1. True, he didn't have to cut a hole in the ice like they do in Alaska, but it's still cold. Though I was invited, I refused to give in to my Catholic guilt and do it for guilt's sake. To me, it didn't prove anything. It may be brave, challenging, and fun, but what would it mean? So, I stood on the side and filmed a Facebook live for them.

While watching them, I thought, "What could I do that would make a substantial difference in my life for my dream?" Though I refused to be guilted, I was inspired by their actions. I couldn't stop thinking, "It's time. I have to do something. If they'll jump into freezing cold water, I can jump back into my dream. Why would I let seven years of effort just sit on my hard drive? Why? Because I don't want to be rejected? Ugh, what kind of a teacher and motivational speaker am I? How dare I? It's time, as they say, to 'Suck it up, buttercup.'"

I felt like I had been spat out on the beach by the whale. I felt bad for giving up on my dream and not inspiring others by example. I needed to head back to my Nineveh. I left Mark's house and drove to my favorite place overlooking Lake Las Vegas and recommitted to my dream, creating the movie that might inspire the eight-year-old dreamer in everyone who watches. And, bonus, I was going to declare it to the world as well. I sat down where I wrote most of the script. And, like two defibrillator paddles all greased up, yelled, "Clear," and the flatline started to beep. My dream was resurrected.

I was so excited while doing the Facebook live that I rambled through the video. Even I couldn't follow what I was saying. I knew I was all-in, again. When I started back to my Nineveh, I was all-in. I re-engaged and started daily live videos and told people what I was up to. I did my seventeen minutes and spoke my truth about not having a clue how I was going to sell my script to Hollywood. Unexpected people would, on occasion, reach out to me and open the door to con-

DON'T BE A HOBBYIST; BE A LOBBYIST FOR YOUR DREAMS.

tacts they knew in Hollywood. It was like a Kevin Bacon effect. People know people, and because I was all-in, people wanted to help me. *Breakthroughs happen when you are all-in.*

This is not about me but about *your* dream. Are you willing to go all-in? I have a motto: Don't be a hobbyist; be a lobbyist for your dreams.

One more example. I hadn't written a book in over a decade and never by myself. When my friend Vince, who had written four books, heard how excited I was about this book and how it all poured out of me in seventeen *days*, he offered to help edit it for me. Again, the underdog effect. I hadn't even asked. He had experience in a place I needed help. Full disclosure: I love to write but have dyslexia, so my writing needs a lot of clean-up. Your excitement, persistence, and commitment will get people to come alongside you, especially in the areas where you need help and they have experience. Keep your eyes open; it will happen.

Are you ready to dive into the chilly waters of the unknown and start touching some sawgrass? Keep answering these questions to stay focused on your mission.

17
YOUR
SEVENTEEN-MINUTE
MISSION

▶ What will achieving your dream feel like?

▶ What if you can still take care of your responsibilities *and* go for it?

▶ What's your Nineveh? What is that whisper of a dream that you keep thinking about?

▶ What can you do to get out of the whale of self-doubt?

▶ Are you stopping you? If you are, then you can stop stopping you.

▶ Do you see the difference in being all-in?

CHAPTER 11

GOT SEVENTEEN MINUTES?

I EARNED A REAL-LIFE doctorate in failure. I transformed from a shy, quiet kid that wasn't funny and physically shook when he stood in front of an audience to standing on stage in front of 2,000 people, making them laugh and becoming the World Champion. A few things worked along the way. Most didn't, but the sawgrass moments were plentiful because I was all-in. Those critical experiences taught this former mommy's boy valuable lessons about the one subject they say you can't learn—being funny. What principles helped me get the breakthroughs I need to achieve that dream, that I could distill it down to a simple strategy that would lead me to my next dream?

This time, though, I can't let the whale of self-doubt stop me as it did in 2019. If I'm going to strive for my next ridiculous movie dream, I need a newly refined strategy.

Do you have seventeen minutes?

Like, if your life depended on it, could you set aside seventeen minutes today?

What if your dream depended on it? Think about it, when you watch a show on a service like Netflix, a typical half-hour show is twenty-two minutes without commercials. An hour show is about forty-four minutes. You probably find time to watch some of those. So, what is your dream worth? Could you give at least seventeen minutes a day for your dream?

If you're honest with yourself, you've often wasted at least that much time. If you hit snooze three times, that's over seventeen minutes. For me, guilty as charged. If you were truly the CEO, you would probably think, "Okay, time to make some changes around here." Say it out loud, even if no one is around.

It's your dream. You're the CEO. Do you have seventeen minutes?

Why seventeen? That's a fair question.

Growing up, I loved sports, but I was far from a gifted athlete. In middle and high school, if I was lucky enough to make the team, I was always second string. I sat on the bench, watching my more talented friends play in the game. I would only get to play if we were way ahead or behind near the end of the game. I *wanted* to be in the game, as every kid did, but the coaches who decided who would play disagreed. Honestly, they were right. Looking back, I didn't deserve it. I did not have natural talent or the drive to develop it. We can *want* with great desire, but that does not get the coaches to *want* you in the game. Wanting to get in the game and doing what it actually takes to get in the game, are very different. Are you just wanting your dream or actually doing what it takes to make actual progress? Something happened the summer before my senior year in high school. I was sick and tired of watching from the sidelines. Enough was enough.

When have you felt that before? You had enough, and game on! You were all-in. That's the feeling we need to get, keep, and know how to access ourselves when we lose our drive. We need that mission mindset. We need to look at our dream as a mission.

I realized my senior year was my last chance to play as a starter. I didn't care what position; I just wanted to be on the field in the action. I hit the weights. I started running four miles a day. I went to a Holy Cross College summer football camp. I did this before my high school team even had our first practice. I had momentum.

When we started practicing, my coaches still had last year's Darren in their heads. Fine. I would show them. I was the first one to practice and the last one to leave the locker room. When we did sprints, I gave it everything I had while some of my teammates worked just hard enough.

When the first game of the season came around, I was still sitting on the bench and watching my friends play. But I was not done. I still kept up my work ethic. Lifting weights was starting to show. People began to notice, which gave me hope and got me to lean in even more. Hope is a critical ingredient to achievement. By the third game of the season, I finally won a starting position as a defensive cornerback and returning punts. I was now in the game.

It was the first time in my life I took 100 percent responsibility and was all-in. I transformed who I was as a player and a person. I was no longer a wimp. I became the player the coaches wanted in the game. I never became a star athlete, but that wasn't my goal. I was no longer standing on the sidelines in a perfectly clean uniform. I'll always remember that feeling and accomplishment. It is a time in my life that I look back on and smile.

My practice jersey was number seventeen. My game jersey was a different number. It's what we do *in practice* that determines *if* we get in the game and how well we do when we get there. It wasn't until I was all-in that the coaches started to notice.

Do you have any experience in your life like that that you can draw on? Start drawing. And, if you don't, maybe now you can create that sawgrass experience.

So, why seventeen minutes? Because it was my practice jersey number. There's no scientific reason. If you have a number that is significant to you, use that. The number of minutes isn't so important. *What is critical is that you start and that you invest the time consistently.* I decided to start focusing on my dream for at least seventeen minutes a day. You can do it. What will you do in those seventeen minutes? Get a book, take a course, do some research, ask people questions who have accomplished the dream you desire. Do *something.* Your time must be focused. Turn your phone on airplane mode if you need to. I set the stopwatch on my phone and go all-in for at least seventeen minutes. My intention is to get caught up in what I'm doing and to keep going. I do not limit myself to seventeen minutes. Whenever possible, more is better.

SEVENTEEN MINUTES IS SHORT ENOUGH TO COMMIT TO DAILY, WHILE BEING LONG ENOUGH TO MAKE PROGRESS.

If you have a number of minutes that resonates with you, commit to it. Seventeen minutes is short enough to commit to daily, while being long enough to make progress. Does that make sense? Even if you are busy or tired, you can squeeze in seventeen minutes. Ask the CEO. I learned that if I committed to an hour a day, I wouldn't do it every day. Some days, I would probably resent having to do it. So, I chose seventeen. It felt manageable. There are days I don't feel like doing it. I do it anyway. There are days I stop as soon as I get to seventeen minutes on my stopwatch. That's okay. I made progress. That makes me feel good.

Before I finally recommitted, I had been depressed. I was down. I did not feel good about myself. I had a hard time pulling myself away from the TV. When I went all-in again, I felt good.

I was excited most days. Even on the not-so-good days, I kept the momentum going. If you feel an ebb and flow in your passion for doing the hard work for your dream, that is normal. Keep going. Ride the wave and keep paddling until you do.

How do you eat an elephant? One bite at a time? Nope. That was the old way. The new plan is at least seventeen minutes per day.

17 YOUR SEVENTEEN-MINUTE MISSION

▶ Do you see the difference in being all-in?

▶ Are you ready for a strategy to help you take care of responsibilities, make progress, overcome doubt, gain momentum and tap into the underdog effect?

▶ So, it's your dream—got seventeen minutes?

▶ Want a daily dose of inspiration? Remember to go to: 365InspirationalQuotes.com

CHAPTER 12

HOW TO BUILD YOUR BELIEF

C AN YOU REMEMBER seeing an excited child rip open the perfect gift? Their eyes grow wide with enthusiasm. The joy lights up their face. When I was growing up, for me, it was a Hot Wheels race track. This was before electric race tracks that whipped the cars around the track. Picture this: An orange track, two fast spinning rubber wheels on each side of the track that grab the cars and catapult them forward around the track. The wheels give the car instant velocity and momentum, but then they gradually slow

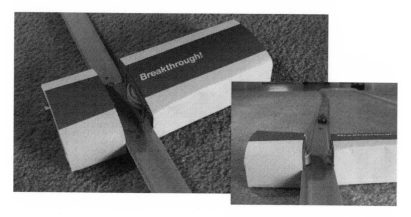

down until they make it back to the spinning wheels again. It's fun for kids. For you and me, it represents our reality.

On our dream journey, we may gradually slow down over time, and so we need momentum boosts. Those "wheels" that propel us forward are our breakthroughs. When we get a breakthrough, we instantly gain velocity and we feel invincible for a while. The breakthrough is an unforgettable lesson learned, gained through experience. After that, we are never the same. The big question is whether we'll have enough momentum and staying power to get us to that next breakthrough. What's sad is that most people give up just before their next breakthrough because they didn't have enough momentum to keep them going.

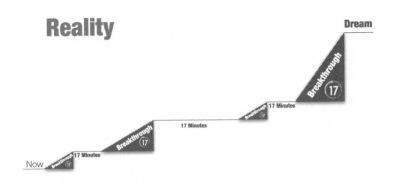

The challenge is we don't know when they are coming. They come at random times and random intervals. Momentum builds belief. That's why it's so critical to build in a regular habit that will produce more consistent breakthroughs. I love the way author Steven Pressfield says it, "This is the other secret that real artists know and wannabe writers don't. When we sit down each day and do our work, power concentrates around us. The Muse takes note of our dedication." What's he saying? Discipline yourself to sit down and put seventeen minutes into your dream every day, and breakthroughs ("The Muse") will happen [S. Pressfield, *The War of Art: Break Through the Blocks and Win Your Inner Creative Battles*, New York, Black Irish Entertainment LLC, 2012].

Here is another interesting example related to this idea. I delivered a presentation at a high-profile building in Washington, DC (which I cannot mention) to a group of Toastmasters. The Toastmaster who had invited me was also a tour guide. It was cool to get a personal tour. During the tour, we walked up some steps outside the building. It felt awkward. The steps were uneven. The heights of each step varied. It was the weirdest sensation I ever had climbing stairs.

Turns out, it was by design, not by accident. The tour guide explained that if a militia ever rushed the building, they could not gain momentum. They were non-momentum steps. When writing this book, I tried googling it but could not find any intel. I bet that is by design as well. Are you planning your success by design or not? If you work on your dream in random intervals, or only when you have the time, you simply won't gain momentum.

This important part of the government recognizes that momentum is uber significant. If you want to achieve your dream, make momentum a top priority.

In the past, I took uneven steps toward my dream of getting a movie made about my story. I've started and stopped, gaining but then losing momentum. This time, I was going to make sure things were different. Some people say the hardest part is getting up and doing something. I say the hardest part is sitting down and focusing. I realized, if that's the hardest part for me, if I could do it, I would make real progress. If I make progress, I will create momentum. If I create momentum, I will build my belief that this dream is possible.

The plan is a seventeen-minute minimum every day. I had days, especially early on, when I surpassed seventeen. Even on the days I was overwhelmed in my business or personal life, I still forced myself to get in my seventeen minutes. When I sent one of my daily screenshots to my accountability buddy, Sara, she sent me this text back: Yep.

My friend Maureen Zappala, a former NASA engineer, reminded me of the scientific formula for momentum. She is brilliant but said momentum is simple to understand. Its symbol is "p," which seems weird for the word momentum. I guess the Germans, who developed the formula, had already used "m," so the "p" comes from the word impulse. The equation is: P = M x V.

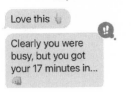

This formula reads, "Momentum equals mass multiplied by velocity." That means momentum will increase when mass and/or velocity increase. Maureen told me, "A daily habit is like velocity; it can be steady and constant. And in those daily commitments, you make more progress, which is like building mass."

My geek friends may have a "geekgasm" over this. You may not be a numbers lover. Either way, this formula can help you build your belief and see your growth. It will show you your truth and help get you out of your way while giving you a sense of accomplishment.

How? Start a simple spreadsheet and track your minutes. If you don't know how to use a spreadsheet, figure it out. You are the CEO; find a way. Watch YouTube videos. You only need a basic one. It can help you build your belief, which is essential to continuing your journey, overcoming doubt, enduring a plateau, and getting to your desired destination.

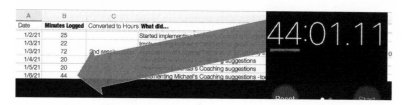

Each day, when I finish my "work on the dream session," I stop my stopwatch and click a screenshot. (If you don't know how to do that, again, find a YouTube video or ask a teenager. No excuses.) I then take my number and enter it into my spreadsheet. These are real numbers from my journey. (I'm a huge fan of inspiring by example. I'm not telling you to do anything I have not done.) One day, I had forty-four minutes. Another day, eighteen minutes. One day, I had one hour and twenty-four minutes. Bam. Progress.

If I committed to an hour a day, I would not be as eager to sit down and focus. When I'm on a roll, it is easy to keep going, and I go well beyond seventeen minutes. The key is sitting down and starting. When I looked at what I logged in my first thirty-one days, I had totaled 1,437 minutes, which equates to 23.95 hours. You can do that too. Your minutes will add up, and your belief will start building.

YOU DON'T KNOW WHICH MINUTES WILL MATTER.

What will you do? Do something, anything. Just get started. New ideas will come to you along the way. Some of my minutes the first month were researching online. Some of my minutes were implementing ideas I got when Michael Hauge coached me. He had given me two pages of improvement ideas, so I sat down each day and improved my script. It was too much to do all at once, so I did it day by day as I put in my daily minutes. And doing it that way helped me to establish my new daily habit and create real momentum.

Here is one of the most important principles in this book: You don't know *which minutes will matter.*

Date	Minutes Logged	Converted to Hours	What did...
1/2/21	25		Started implementing Michael's Coaching suggestions
1/3/21	22		Implementing Michael's Coaching suggestions
1/3/21	72	2nd session today	Watched Credits/Special Features of "I Can Only Imagine" (Erwin Brothers and took notes for Top 100
1/4/21	20		Implementing Michael's Coaching suggestions
1/5/21	20		Implementing Michael's Coaching suggestions
1/6/21	44		Implementing Michael's Coaching suggestions -today (48-1) to (50-1)
1/7/21	18		Implementing Michael's Coaching suggestions (53-1) (60-1) (62-1)
1/8/21	17		Implementing Michael's Coaching suggest (65-1) (65-2)
1/9/21	46		emailed Brian Ivie & Reviewed his trailer
1/10/21	30		Implementing Michael's Coaching MH Coaching (66-1)(67-2)(72-1)(73-1)
1/11/21	75		Implemented the rest of Mich ay (96-1) to (122-1)
1/12/21	84		Started list of Top 100 and suggestions, reseached a bit and sent script to Brian Ivie
1/13/21	69		Sent fb message to Jon research (I was really scared sending it) LinkedIN Research Too
1/14/21	44		Sent fb message to Kevin Downes
1/15/21	50		Spoke to Shell as and sent her script.
1/16/21	53		Watch the ma and did some research
1/17/21			Wrote Shelley scene) In Darren 2
1/18/21	38		Found Butch's spec was produced by Sean Mcnamara (Soul Surfer - talked to Roxann about her contact
1/19			Spoke to Butch Bradley about movie and his connection to Sean
	28		More research and sent a fb message to David A. R. White

You honestly don't know which minutes will matter. For example, on the eighteenth day of my recommitment, I put in thirty-eight minutes. That's it. It's not a lot, but on that day, I was gathering intel on the producers and directors of movies like mine; because if somehow I can get them to be aware of my story, maybe they would consider telling it. One of the names on my list was Sean McNamara. I couldn't find in my notes which movie he had directed. So, I jumped on IMDB.com and looked him up. Turns out, he had directed *Soul Surfer* in 2011. I just happened to be curious as to the other films he directed. I slowly scrolled up the list. When I got to the top of the list, Mr. McNamara had directed an Amazon Prime special called *Butch Bradley: From Las Vegas.*

Butch Bradley was a friend of mine. He and I did standup comedy together back in Boston. He had been a guest on my

Unforgettable Presentations podcast. I was in the audience when they filmed the show last year. I immediately called Butch and left him a message. After we chatted, Butch reached out for me and got an email address and permission to send the script to Mr. McNamara's team.

At the time of this writing, I have not heard anything back. And I don't know if anything will come of it, but it might. And I do know this: It gave me a burst of hope. To me, it felt like a God wink. Especially at the beginning of your journey, hope is critical. Collect and document anything that gives you hope along the way. It builds belief. If you have bad days, you can go back and lean on it.

Consider this: *Resolve to evolve.*

This is your life. You are the CEO. You might be wondering how? These are the steps:

1. Get direction (From a qualified source)

2. Apply it (Touch the sawgrass)

3. Correction (Adjust or get from a qualified source)

4. Repeat

Back in 1992, when I decided I would try standup, I had been inundating myself with motivational tapes. I heard a common theme was to go to people who were the best because they think differently and give advice from experience. When I decided to give it a shot, I went to my first comedy club and asked the headliner that night for advice. He told me to get a book. It wasn't just any book. It was a book recommended by a guy in the arena. That is a *qualified* direction.

You can take a class (which is direction), which is good, but it's not enough. We need to take that direction and actually apply it to internalize the insight to become a part of who we are. At my trademarked Humor Boot Camp, I teach presenters how to create humor customized to their audience that they can use again and again. Part of the training is breaking down the structure of stories and jokes. They leave understanding comedy principles, and they will never look at humor the same way again.

During the boot camp, we suggest they study their favorite comedians. It would be powerful if they took this seriously. If you wish to transform, you must be all-in. Many people are perpetual students. After taking a class or reading a book, they are done. No—now you need to go apply it.

Pankaja Kalabkar took the Humor Boot Camp virtually from India. She is a sponge. She sent me this WhatsApp chat message that said:

She was doing her minutes. The minutes after any workshop, conference, or class can be game-changers for you. We want you to internalize the new insights. When you internalize them, they become a part of you. Many others took the same Humor Boot Camp as Pankaja, but she took more from it than most because she did her minutes after the direction. She had the experience of applying what she learned.

When we apply what we learn, it's more likely to bring us a breakthrough. Part of the reason is it now gets into your subconscious mind. The conscious mind is what we think about, but the subconscious mind is where we operate and where our habits lay. One of my success coaches, Dawn Nocera, brilliantly told me, "An aha moment is the letting go of a previous belief."

I hope that was an aha for you. It was for me. Think about it. Achieving our dreams usually requires many aha moments along the way. We can't just think about them, we must also internalize them to become a part of who we are. As you do, who you are transforms.

Nothing is guaranteed, but if you do at least seventeen minutes a day, you will make progress. Progress leads to breakthroughs; breakthroughs lead to results; results build belief. With belief and hope, nothing can stop you but you.

One of my favorite motivators is Rudy Ruettiger, the man behind the movie, *Rudy*. He said, "People aren't afraid of hard work; they are afraid of hard work not paying off."

YOUR
SEVENTEEN-MINUTE
MISSION

▶ Will you get your direction from a qualified source?

▶ You don't know which minutes will matter.

▶ Track your progress, and you'll build your belief.

▶ Building your momentum builds belief: P = M x V.

▶ Start your spreadsheet, or download mine. Go to
17Minutestoyourdream.com/download.

▶ Can you visualize the spinning wheels on the race track?
See how that relates to your journey?

CHAPTER 13

NOW LET'S DRAMATICALLY UP YOUR SUCCESS RATE

BEFORE YOU DIVE all-in, remember this: "No one becomes world-class alone." You need a team. You must be super careful who is on it. Your team choice could make or break your chances. The cool thing is, as CEO, you can trade, fire, and upgrade your team at any time. They will either fuel your fire or throw water on your flames. There is no room for middle ground on your team.

Team? Yep, your board of directors. The cool thing is it's pretty simple, and it won't cost you anything. You will be doing them a huge service. If you follow this strategy, you could positively impact their lives. More about that in a minute.

I suggest you choose two accountability buddies. Their role is simple. They agree to let you send them screenshots of your daily stopwatch. Choose people you trust who will not be critics and will be encouraging. But they need to be people who will keep you honest.

I'd suggest you sit down with them in person or at least on a video call. Have a discussion about your why. Let them know why this matters to you. It will go a long way to having them come alongside you and cheer you on.

When I first started this, I chose my friends Sheri and Sara. I didn't think it through at the time, but I knew them both well, and they were a great choice. What I didn't see coming was the bonus side effect. We affect people around us for the good and bad. If you hung around your closest friends who all ate fast food daily, would you be more or less likely to eat fast food? If you spent a lot of time with close friends who worked out and ate healthily, would you be more or less likely to work out and eat healthily? We might have a great deal of willpower, but our close friends and family eventually influence us.

After seventy-seven days of daily text images to Sara and Sheri, I realized my consistency and commitment impacted them. I asked my accountability buddies how my actions affected their thoughts about their journeys.

Sheri Broussard told me:

> *It's been incredibly inspiring. The part about it that has been the most inspiring is the fact that you showed up every day. Regardless of if you felt like it, had a perfect message, you were tired, sad…whatever. You said you were gonna do it and you did it. It's powerful. Most people, as we know, NEVER keep promises to themselves. They come up with lame excuses as to why they can't do what they said they'd do. The seventy-seven-day challenge is a practice in promise keeping and it's the practice that can be used toward any and all goals. Even though I didn't do it myself, I was watching, and it was very inspiring.*

Sara McGill told me:

Being on the receiving end of an accountability partnership, like I was for Darren, actually encouraged me to start setting my own daily goals. Each day he would send a screenshot of the time he spent working on his goal whether it was hours or just minutes. On the days it was hours, it made me think about clearing my own calendar to make more time for my own goals. (Which I did!) On the days it was just minutes, I remember thinking, "Wow, just eighteen minutes. He must have been really busy today, but he still squeezed in the time to work toward his goals." Those days especially reminded me that even huge tasks or goals can be accomplished with small, consistent time commitments every single day.

In his autobiography, The Big Sea, *Langston Hughes*

said, "The only way to get a thing done is to start to do it, then keep doing it, and finally you'll finish it."

Nothing could describe Darren's Seventeen Minutes Concept better than that. I used the Seventeen Minutes concept to finish different areas of my website. I committed to working on specific pages or sections for just seventeen minutes a day until those areas were finished. It worked! Some days I ended up working for hours and finishing up more than the one section I had planned to do. Other days I got the minimum done, but I was still moving forward toward finishing my website. I still have more to do, but my website is finally looking professional thanks to my small, consistent time commitment each day.

I'll be transparent: I did not see that one coming. I was asking them a favor that took just a little time and zero effort on their part. When you are all-in, you will affect the world and the people around you.

You may also upset some of your friends who are secretly jealous of you taking responsibility for your dream. Some people don't want to be CEO of their life and dreams because that would mean they can't blame their lack of success on others. Some are comfortable living life that way.

Caution: Do not tell your victim friends what you are doing until you have an established habit. You need to set your trajectory for liftoff. Even then, you may not want to tell others who are negative. When people start asking you, "What's different about you?" Take that as a ginormous win. Then smile and ask them if they have seventeen minutes.

17 YOUR SEVENTEEN-MINUTE MISSION

▶ Who will be your accountability buddies?

▶ Have a conversation with them and tell them your why.

▶ What if you inspired them with your *all-in intelligence*?

▶ Start your 77-Day-Challenge Tracker spreadsheet or download mine. Go to 17Minutestoyourdream.com/download.

CHAPTER 14

SEVENTY-SEVEN-DAY CHALLENGE (I DOUBLE-DOG DARE YOU!)

IT WAS IN the middle of one of my big speaker's conferences in March 2019. I was listening to one of my copresenters and mentors, Patricia Fripp. She had the audience mesmerized. Since I'm in charge of the event, my brain was focused on keeping things running smoothly. Then she said it. It hit me like a cold, wet slap across the face. She said, "Tell me what you say you want. Show me one week of your life, and we will both know if you will achieve it." Brilliant. I looked around to make sure our conference attendees caught that brilliance. I wondered if they understand the depths of that wisdom.

Deep down inside, I started processing what she said. I think my brain had the pinwheel of death you see when your computer can't keep up.

I had been telling people about the script I was writing. I have to admit that I liked the reaction I got when I told people about my big crazy dream. I had to ask myself: Was I settling for the reaction? Was the buzz I got by impressing people with the idea of writing a screenplay taking the place of actually writing it?

I mean, I had been writing it. But I had been writing it…for *seven years*.

Also, once I finished it, I then had to sell it to someone in Hollywood. That meant I would have to face rejection. That's not fun. So, if I didn't finish it, I wouldn't have to get to the scary part. Maybe that's part of the reason I was going so slow?

If you don't know, a standard Hollywood script is 120 pages. After seven years of working on the script, I only had 81 pages completed. Let's do the math: 365 x 7 = 2,555 days, divided by 81 pages, means I completed 0.037 percent of a page per day. Yikes.

Patricia's brilliance woke me up. No one becomes world-class or accomplishes anything major without consistent progress, a.k.a. momentum.

I needed to hear Patricia say those words. And I needed to apply what she said. It was time to make some changes. I did. Here were my results:

The Momentum Difference

My example:

Once a week *7 years* = *81 pages*

Once a day *4 months* = *51 pages*

How about you?

I decided to put in daily work on my dream. Want to know what happened? It had taken me seven years to write eighty-one pages. Then, because of establishing a daily habit, I wrote another fifty-one pages in a matter of a few months.

You can't gain momentum occasionally. Remember the high school physics lesson: A body at rest tends to stay at rest. A body in motion tends to stay in motion. Friction is what slows it down. We must keep applying effort. What if I acted on Patricia's insight years ago?

Please get this: You need to do it daily. Remember the story about the first-time comedian who crushed it? And, that I had been struggling to get just a few laughs in my five minutes? I will never forget that I hung my head low and was completely deflated. Then my comedy mentor, Vinnie, answered my question, "How do you know who is going to make it and who is not?" He laughed and said, "That's simple. Whoever keeps going." Yes, you've heard that before in this book. It is too important to not mention a second time because it was a game-changer. Please remember that simple wisdom. Will you keep going?

Because of his words, I knew that I had to keep going. The same is true for you and it's about to get real. I'm going to double-dog dare you. I challenge you to make *at least* seventeen minutes of progress per day toward your dream for seventy-seven days. Hopefully, like me, you will be on a roll and do many more minutes.

Why seventy-seven days? Back in 2001, when I reached the highest level of the speech contest, I had seventy-seven days until the World Championship Public Speaking Contest. The rules say that you must create a completely new speech for the finals. I had seventy-seven days to create a brand-new speech from scratch. I worked the hardest I had ever worked, and I got a coach, Mark Brown, a former World Champion. I was all-in.

Because I was all-in and had a world-class coach, I didn't just write a new speech—I transformed who I was as a speaker and a person. I had so many unexpected breakthroughs that I was never the same. I believe if you go all-in for seventy-seven days, you can get the breakthroughs you need, expected and unexpected. I asked some of my students if they had a similar experience during their seventy-seven-day challenge. Actually, they did, and their stories are worth hearing.

Does that sound exciting? Yes, of course, but a word of caution is necessary. If you are a podcaster, chances are you have heard the term "podfade." It means that podcasters are enthusiastic when they launch, but many never make it past their seventh episode without their motivation fading.

When we launched our *Unforgettable Presentations* podcast, I was aware of the concept and protected our podcast against it. My cohost Mark Brown and I committed that we would put out an episode each week and keep each other accountable. Awareness of the possibility of podfade assured that we didn't make the mistake of allowing it to happen to us.

What does that have to do with you? If you're anything like me, I get excited and make emotional decisions, dive in, and then eventually my enthusiasm fades.

Enthusiasm is good; consistency is better. Both are best and might even make you unstoppable. As my friend and marketing guru Cathey Armillas says, "Consistency beats ability." Think about that. When we are the underdog, like **BEWARE OF** I was, we need principles like this to fuel our **DREAM FADE!** fire.

As a former World Champion of Public Speaking, speakers come to me for advice. Many times, I have seen ego-filled intention. I get it. My coach Mark Brown had to talk me off the ego ledge. When people come to me with confidence, but they aren't willing to do the work because they think, "I've got this," I tell them, "There is someone out there half as good as you, working twice as hard."

If you are the underdog, then be the person willing to work twice as hard as anyone else, and no one can count you out. You will have good days. You will have bad days. You will have breakthrough days. You will have days when you feel like you went backward. That is part of any dream journey. Congratulations, you are human.

What can happen in seventy-seven days? In June 2001, I had won five levels of the International Speech Contest, and I was going to the finals. I had to write a new speech. I had met World Champion Mark Brown that day and asked him to coach me on my final speech. He agreed. A couple of weeks later, I drove over two hours to work with my coach for the first time. Keep in mind, at this point in my career I had been speaking and doing comedy since 1992. I was a part-time professional keynote speaker. I was animated and had confidence on stage.

Mark guided me on how to write my next speech from scratch. I went deep into my life. When I arrived in the small corporate theater, I handed Mark the first version of my speech. As I handed him the speech, I swore it was so good you could hear choirs of angels singing in the background. I figured if he could give me those tiny tweaks it needed, it would be amazing. I was so proud of what I wrote.

Mark looked over the speech. Concern started to cover his face. He flipped to page two, and he started shaking his head. I started getting defensive. He looked me dead in the eye and, with as much kindness as he could muster, said, "Oh, Darren. We have some work to do." I thought, "Work? What? This is the best I've got!"

He must have forgotten how good I was on stage. What about my passion? These are just words on a page—what did he mean?

After I calmed down and took a few minutes to shut down my ego, I learned one of the most valuable lessons of my life: If you aren't coachable, there is no cure.

Please get this: I had confidence on stage, but I wasn't saying much. I did not have world-class content, and my ego was in the way. I thought I had written the speech I wanted to present, but in spite of what I believed at the time, there was much more work left to do.

IF YOU AREN'T COACHABLE, THERE IS NO CURE.

If you have already achieved your dream and are living the life you have wanted, you probably wouldn't be interested in this book. If not, then think about what's between where you are now and where you want to be. That would come to light for me in the seventy-seven days with Mark Brown.

There are false beliefs and insecurities many of us carry with us from our youth. We need to transform and get our breakthroughs to accomplish our dreams. I needed to change my skills on stage, my self-beliefs, my writing, and even who I was. Seventy-seven days later, under the most pressure of my life, I delivered a speech that not only won the contest, but which people are still talking about two decades later.

I'm not saying that to brag. I'm saying it because I transformed who I was in *seventy-seven days*. I believe if you are all-in, you can too. It takes being all-in to transform. To be all-in, I had to have great coaches, work daily on my speech, and say a lot of prayers. Please understand, even if I had not won the contest, I would never be the same presenter or person I was seventy-seven days prior. I like to remind people, "If you took away my struggle, you would take away my growth." So, with the strategy used to achieve my first dream, I press on now to accomplish the steps that will help actualize my second dream.

On this next journey toward my dream of writing a successful script and having it made into a movie, here are my minutes after seventy-seven days:

- I have logged 4,324 minutes, equal to 72.07 hours.

- I have not sold my script yet.

- I am not the same person now as when I started this new journey.

- I have a much-improved script, more contacts, many breakthroughs, more confidence, and for sure, more belief in myself than I did when I recommitted.

I have momentum toward achieving my second dream.

Do you want to increase the momentum toward your dream?

I double-dog dare you. I'm challenging you to dive all-in for seventy-seven days. After seventy-seven days, pop your head up and look back and see if you are not in a much different place than when you started. I'd be willing to bet you have created some new relationships and maybe put some other draining ones on the back burner. Notice if any unexpected connections and coincidences have occurred. Look back and congratulate yourself on your growth. Then, you as the CEO of your dream can choose to keep going.

I can't tell you specifically what to do for your dream. You'll have to get some direction from qualified experts in that area. Seek out books, courses, and mentors. I needed many along my way.

Reminder: Back in my standup comedy days, I learned from

many Boston headliners that any day you don't go on stage is a day that you don't grow. What? Yep. There is usually one foundational habit in an area that is critical to growth toward your dream. At the beginning, I spent much of my time seeking stage time. In the beginning of a comedian's career, no one wants to give you stage time because you are horrible. So, in the beginning, stage time is limited to open-mic nights until you prove yourself.

For my students striving to be world-class presenters, I challenged them to do a short live video every day. Even though it is not in front of an audience, it would train them to get comfortable talking into a lens. I had no idea how critical this would be during the pandemic when speakers were left speechless. I told my students it didn't matter if the live video was on Facebook, Instagram, YouTube, LinkedIn, or any other platform.

I did that "one live video a day" challenge myself to lead by example. We can all enhance our skills. I have done that challenge each year for three years. The first year I did it, it was a ninety-day challenge. I'm so grateful I have been able to inspire others to do the same. One of my students recently reached out to me and told me how much the challenge helped her. Jennifer Haston said:

Hi there. I'm Jennifer Haston of The Professor Helps and I am so excited to tell you about the daily video challenge that coach, Darren LaCroix put us on a couple of years ago because it terrified me at the time. The 90-Day Challenge was you get online, and you post a message and there wasn't a time limit given. You just had to at least do a minute and talk about what matters to you. And it's led to amazing

*things. For me, it led me to a dream job. It led me
to my own podcast, and it led me to start a YouTube
channel. And it would not have happened, none of
it would've happened, without the encouragement of
Darren and the ninety-day challenge.*

I love to hear that. I only gave Jennifer the challenge (direction). She is the one who did the work (application). She got the aha moments. She had the breakthroughs. She got results.

Do you want results?

I hope you see how you have gained momentum while transforming and building your beliefs. So much so that you keep going until you achieve your dream. An advertising slogan I love says, "Progress is perfection." I wished I'd thought of it.

Heads up, you may have an occasional "hiccup day," a day that you miss. A day nothing happens. Take a screenshot of 0:00 and send it to your accountability buddy. Don't let it bother you. Worse, don't let it stop your momentum. It's just a hiccup, but keep going.

Reminder: You don't know which minutes will matter. When I was doing my daily video challenge with my students, I received great unexpected bonuses. Many days, I did not want to do the video. One day, I was exhausted from delivering four virtual keynotes the day before. I did it anyway. I've learned, by sawgrass experience, that we often connect more deeply on those days. One new member, Richard, sent us a message right after joining: "I saw Darren's seventy-seven-day video challenge the day he was looking and feeling rough and did the video anyway. I was impressed with his dedication to power through and decided I want to work with someone who is that committed."

Often, those minutes that we don't think matter are the ones that matter the most. One night, I was trying to be creative and feeling a bit wacky. I decided to put my phone on my ceiling fan and jump up and down on my bed as I was recording. I'm sure I had a point in my head, but it did not come through clearly, and that's okay! I later found out Ms. Eager Emerging Speaker (who does not wish to be named) was watching. She sent a Facebook message: "Thank goodness for those Facebook lives of yours (even the bed-jumping one) cause without 'em, I would never have discovered you."

Remember that free training I mentioned at the beginning of the book, where two people were brutal critics? Ms. Emerging Speaker ended up going through that same Get Paid to Speak training and joined my business mastery program. What if I didn't do my bed-jumping video that day? Those minutes mattered. I may not have gained a new client.

What if you don't do your minutes? What breakthroughs might you miss? Remember, regrets suck.

Whether you are a believer or not, there are some truths in the Bible. This passage helps me to keep swinging when I feel like my effort was already good enough. Consider 2 Kings 13:18–19:

> *Elisha continued, "Get some arrows." So, the king did. Elisha told him, "Strike the ground." Jehoash struck it three times. Then he stopped. The man of God was angry with him. He said, "You should have struck the ground five or six times. Then you would have won the war over Aram. You would have completely destroyed them. But now you will win only three battles over them."*

Keep swinging.

17 YOUR SEVENTEEN-MINUTE MISSION

▶ You don't know which minutes will matter.

▶ Keep striking the ground.

▶ Go all-in for seventy-seven days.

▶ Test me on this.

▶ Beware of dream fade.

▶ Start your 77-Day-Challenge Tracker spreadsheet or download mine. Go to 17Minutestoyourdream.com/download.

CHAPTER 15

LISTEN FOR THE WEIRD WHISPERS

'M NOT GOING to lie to you. This may sound a little weird, but it's real. I want to encourage you to visualize your preferred future and say daily affirmations that proclaim core truths you want to embrace and that will help you move to your preferred future. Here's the weird part: When you do these visualizations and affirmations, you may get to hear little whispers and feel gentle nudges. Yeah, I told you it was weird, and on the surface, it makes no logical sense. But it's true. Or at least it's true for me.

I think it's important to realize you don't know the precise path to your dreams. You also don't know exactly what you need to have on your journey with you. One of our critical tasks is listening and being open. You may get a nudge or an idea. You can call it your subconscious mind, spirit, the universe, or God. The idea may not make sense. Do it anyway.

I'm not asking you to do anything immoral or illegal. I am asking you to be willing to be uncomfortable, stretch yourself, and realize that while it may not completely make sense at that moment, it may make sense down the road.

When I was all-in back in 2001 and working on my speech, I also wrote out affirmations and visualizations. I clearly remember one morning when I was focused, and a random thought popped into my head, "You need to run four miles a day." What? What does that have to do with giving a speech? At the moment, it made zero sense.

A few days later, I thought about it. It started to make sense. When delivering a speech, who you are matters. When you are under stress, like, in a world championship speech contest, handling stress is critical. I needed to be in the best shape of my life. Running daily allowed me to use my stress to help me better prepare to handle stress.

There is much more to achieving a dream than meets the eye. It is not all completely logical. The ideas that come to you may seem weird. When working on my current dream, I got the nudge to go on IMBD to search Sean McNamara. I had the information I needed elsewhere but followed the nudge. It led to a huge dose of hope, which, at the time, I greatly welcomed.

Another thought that hit me, seemingly from left field, was about affirmations. Some of the ones I had written down were from the Bible. I call them "Godfirmations." The idea hit me that I needed to record them to listen to when I fall asleep and wake up. If I'm going to transform who I am, I need to be more careful about my thoughts. It's curious because one of my students said to me, "I feel like you are on a roll, and you are taking all of us with you." Interesting, because only a few weeks before, I felt down. Now, I feel like I'm on a mission. It's a good place to be.

I also got the nudge to make a YouTube video for the directors

I wanted to bring my script to life. It makes no sense. I'm doing it anyway. I can't tell you if or how it will pay off. Why? Because I don't know yet. But I'm following the nudge. I'm listening to the weird whispers. Will you?

Another cool reason to track your minutes on a spreadsheet is so you can look back and track which minutes some of your breakthroughs were born. This will also help you tell your story if you ever choose. It could also help you write a book about your experience. You'll have some important moments plotted. Your spreadsheet will help you tell your story.

17 YOUR SEVENTEEN-MINUTE MISSION

▶ Will you listen to the whispers and nudges?

▶ Will you act on them even if they don't make sense?

▶ Want a daily dose of inspiration? Remember to go to: 365InspirationalQuotes.com

CHAPTER 16

FAITH, LACK, AND YOUR LITTLE CELEBRATIONS

W HEN I LOOK back at some of the simple, practical things
that have worked for me, I think of faith and CDs. If
you are younger than thirty and reading this, you may
have to Google "CDs."

Faith matters. Trust matters. Beliefs matter. For people like
me, it can be a struggle if we have a deep-seated "lack" mentality.
It can be a challenge to overcome. I grew up in a Roman Catholic
family. I'm thankful for my family but now disagree with some
of what I was taught growing up. But that is for another book. I
certainly had insecurities of which I was unaware.

In the late 1990s, I remember getting down on my knees,
asking for God's help as I had plateaued in my career and didn't
seem to be making any progress. I told God I'd start tithing
(giving 10 percent of my income toward the work being done
in His kingdom), even though I was not making much, and my
career seemed to be going nowhere. I promised that if I could

speak for a living, He could do what He wanted with me after that. I trusted Him. I had faith, but I can't say it made sense. Unbeknownst to me at the time, the only time in the Bible where God says to test Him is on tithing.

Even if you are not a believer in God, I hope you have faith in something. When it comes to pursuing dreams, I believe faith matters.

My dream was to be a full-time professional keynote speaker. When I still had my day job, living at home, paying off my business debt and school loans on my telemarketing salary and commissions, I did something right. Deep in debt and struggling, I needed little highlights along the way to keep me going. Money and debt were always on my mind. The only thing that scared me more was going on stage the next time.

I wish I remember where I got this idea, but I think it must have been one of my motivational tapes. Like most people, I loved music. I was a huge fan of Bruce Springsteen, Boston, and Van Halen. I made a pact with myself that for every paid speech I booked, I would tithe 10 percent and buy myself a CD. Tithing helps battle that lack mentality, and the CD was a little celebration. I disciplined myself only to buy a CD when I booked a gig. If I did a $50 comedy gig, I would give $5 to God and buy a CD. When I booked a $500 speech, I gave $50 to God, and I would buy a Van Halen CD.

The cool thing is that the music on those CDs reached me deeply. They moved me. It wasn't just a CD. It was a victory. It was a celebration. I cherished each one. It was a little bit of money and a little celebration, but as my CD collection grew, so did my belief. All the rest of my income went directly to pay down my debt. It was a good plan that worked for me.

What could your celebrations be? It needs to work for you so that you can deny yourself until you hit your mark. Promises to yourself are truly character-developing. You are the CEO. How about celebrating your minute milestones (1,000, 17,000)? You choose. It's your dream. We need to know what motivates us.

Ideas to spoil yourself from some of my friends:

- Hot fudge sundae or favorite dessert
- Dinner at your favorite restaurant (The food will taste better that night)
- See a movie in a theater
- Take a hike
- Buy or download a new book
- Take a scenic drive
- Manicure or pedicure
- Shopping spree
- Massage
- Buy/send yourself flowers or _____
- Staycation
- Buy your pet a new toy
- New pair of shoes
- Special bubble bath—go all out with candles and make your bathroom a spa
- Buy yourself pompoms and give yourself a cheer

My friend Tanya Murray is in real estate. When I asked her, she said when she was first getting started selling homes, she would buy herself a "closing gift." She said it would be something she would not otherwise splurge on. The wonderful bonus is that now, years later, when she looks at her gifts, they reminded her of the clients that she got to know so well during the process and her job well done. For you, how about "breakthrough gifts" or "minute milestone gifts?"

I suggest, whatever you decide, make it mean something. If you don't know right now, think about it. An idea will come. Don't engage in that activity at all *until* it's to celebrate a win. For example, if you choose a hot fudge sundae every time you hit one thousand minutes, then don't have any hot fudge sundaes at any other time. Make it matter more.

YOUR
SEVENTEEN-MINUTE
MISSION

▶ Remember: Your momentum is critical to your dream:
P = M x V

▶ How will you celebrate?

▶ Your celebrations need to have meaning and motivate you.

▶ Tracking can lead to celebrations. Get one step closer
today. If you haven't already, start your 77-Day-
Challenge Tracker spreadsheet or download mine. Go to
17Minutestoyourdream.com/download.

▶ If a better idea comes along that is a better fit and more
motivating, you can change it. Remember, you are the
CEO of your dream.

CHAPTER 17

THE UGLY YELLOW TIE

EVER HAVE A lesson from a teacher that still serves you today? Back before I dreamed of being a comedian, I wanted to become an actor. I had always loved movies and TV and thought it would be the coolest job in the world. I took acting and auditioning classes in the early 1990s when I lived about an hour outside Boston.

I was a sponge back then. And a teacher's pet. I even helped my acting teacher, Bob North, move his furniture. He ended up getting me in a reenactment of an old TV show, *Real Stories of the Highway Patrol*. It was my first paid acting job and a blast. I was in a couple of low, low-budget B movies, and I was in heaven on the set.

One of the things Bob said to me was, "There will be a day when you are tired of going to audition after audition because it feels like nothing ever pans out. That day that you are going to quit is the same day you would have landed the role."

I thought, "That was nice, but I'm never going to quit. I love this." I hoped the other people, who were not as committed as me, were listening. At the time, I had the perfect job to pursue acting. As a telemarketer, I had a somewhat flexible schedule as long as I got my hours in each week.

I lived in central Massachusetts and worked in Framingham, about forty minutes outside of Boston. When I got an audition in the city, I could clock out for an extended lunch, drive to the audition, then drive back to work and extend my day to get the hours in.

One day, I got a call for a big audition for a commercial for Konica. I was excited and took an extended lunch break to make it happen. Sitting in the hallway crammed with actors outside of the casting agency, I was getting antsy. The audition times were way behind. I had flexible hours, but I had thought I'd be back soon. They were over an hour behind. I thought about how many fruitless auditions I had done. Actors were slowly coming out, and those in front of me were heading in. It felt like it was taking forever. It was coming up on ninety minutes. I started thinking I was wasting my time.

Then, another actor popped in the hallway door and walked over to the check-in. He seemed to have a rapport with the agent. She took him next. I thought, "What? Are you kidding me?" I went up and asked how he got in ahead of us. The agent calmly explained that this actor was on break from work and needed to get back. I said, "I am on break too and drove from Framingham as well!" I went back to my seat, and that was it. I was done. It wasn't fair. At that moment, Bob's advice popped into my head, reminding me the day I wanted to quit was the same day I'd land the role.

I thought, "What if Bob is right? I'm here. I'm already going to be late getting back to work. I may lose some brownie points from my boss for taking much longer than expected, but I will stick this last one out. Ugh."

When it finally became my audition, I was standing in front of one of the directors for one of the biggest production companies in Boston. The role was an office guy making photocopies for a hubcap company. They were looking for facial reactions. Something clicked between the director and me. My expressions cracked him up. I could tell he was loving what I was doing. I had a blast.

Sure enough, I got the call. I landed the role. Bob was right. When we filmed the commercial, the wardrobe lady dressed me up and made a custom ugly yellow tie with hubcaps. My character had worked for a hubcap company. After we were done filming, I asked her if I could take the tie home with me. She reluctantly agreed. It hangs in my office now as my constant reminder that the days we will give up are the same days we would get the break-throughs we need.

Thank you, Bob North, wherever you are. Your spot-on lesson still serves me today. Now, more importantly, I hope it serves *you*. We have to pass onto others the lessons of our lives.

I bet you have a similar story. If you do, hold it tight to your heart and remind yourself of your own ugly yellow tie story.

17 YOUR SEVENTEEN-MINUTE MISSION

▶ The ugly yellow tie still hangs in my office as a reminder.

▶ The day you want to give up, remember Bob's wisdom.

▶ What if you need to get to the brink of quitting to get the breakthrough you need?

▶ We all need inspiration from time to time. Want a daily dose? Remember to go to: 365InspirationalQuotes.com.

CHAPTER 18

SEVENTEEN-MINUTE RESULTS

DO YOU HAVE any friends who are health nuts? Maybe you are that friend. My friend Mike is super healthy. When he moved to Las Vegas and we started hanging out, I heard a lot about his passion for nutrition. He was explaining to me, in detail, the devastating effects of too much sugar. I love my coffee in the morning, and being from Boston, I'm a Dunkin' coffee fan. He convinced me that I needed to cut back on my sugar intake. OK, I committed. I'd start having my coffee with just cream. If you are reading this and think the cream is still too much, stick with me here (baby steps).

It was kind of gross, but I was committed. A few days later it was still gross and I felt like it lacked taste. I stuck with it, though. A couple of weeks later, I pulled up to the drive-through and ordered my half calf with just cream. (If you are not from the East coast, that means half regular, half decaffeinated). It smelled amazing. As I took my first sip, I just about spewed the coffee all over my windshield! Blah! They put a ton of sugar in it!

I did not order any. My second reaction was, "Cool!" I did not notice my own transformation along the way. My taste pallet had changed. I can't believe I could drink it that way. It was a health-changing breakthrough. I had more energy, and I was never the same. My friend Amanda Mae Gray says, "You can't notice your own progress in the middle of your progress."

I got this text message as I was finishing up this book. My friend Chic was taking the challenge. He told me it was changing his life! What? When I asked him how it was changing his life,

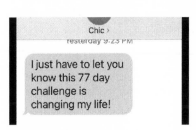

he said that it helped him clarify his message and sharpened his ability to deliver in a more conversational style. He also went on to tell me that the comments he had been getting from people watching his videos blew him away. He had much more impact than he could have imagined. I surmise his confidence went through the roof. Breakthroughs happen when you consistently immerse yourself in the sawgrass experience..

Though my dream now is to bring an inspirational blockbuster movie to life, my current business is being a mentor and a coach to emerging professional presenters. We help good presenters become unforgettable. These are speakers, authors, and coaches who wish to become world-class and get paid to speak.

Each year I run an event called "Game Changers." I force myself to stretch by creating new content each year since we have many attendees return. This idea of seventeen minutes started as a keynote speech I gave to open the conference. I had committed to seventeen minutes a day and thought I'd challenge my students to take the challenge with me.

I learned from my comedy mentors that the critical habit to growing your comedy skills was stage time. Remember I was told that any day that you don't get on stage is a day that you don't grow? Simple, but not easy.

Many of my Stage Time University members have backgrounds like mine in Toastmasters, a place to get stage time when you're just starting. It's a great idea, but most Toastmasters only get an opportunity to deliver a prepared presentation once every other month. If delivering the presentation is a key to growth, doing it every other month will never get them to world-class. That's why I joined *four* Toastmaster clubs as soon as I discovered it. I would go to Toastmasters during the day and comedy clubs at night. I thought, with excitement, *I can fail twice a day.* If that was the key to growth, then that was what I needed to do.

For my students at Stage Time University, their dream is to be world-class presenters. So, I challenged them to do one live video a day to their favorite social media platform—Facebook live, Instagram live, or YouTube live, their choice. The point is that it is live, not filming thirty-two takes and then uploading the best take. Nope. You don't get to do that when giving paid keynote presentations. It is that sawgrass experience right at their fingertips.

We even created a hashtag together: #77DayVideoChallenge. Feel free to go check it out. When I saw so many people jump into the challenge, I was inspired. As I prepared my keynote speech for our event, Game Changers, I thought it might be powerful if I sat down and interviewed them on the mistakes, growth, and breakthroughs they were getting as a result of doing their daily videos (also known as daily minutes).

What they had to say and the breakthroughs they received were so inspiring that it led me to write this book. Keep in mind as you read this, their dream is around speaking, inspiring others, and building their business. My dream is to get the movie on the big screen. The paths are different, but the same daily progress yields movement. I hope these sawgrass experiences inspire you to dive all-in and get your results. They didn't know which minutes would matter. Because they were all-in, they got noticed by me. That is the underdog effect!

Your seventy-seven-day challenge may not need you to do a daily video. My selling a script to Hollywood requires reaching out and pitching my idea to people of influence. Your dream may require different daily minutes to get the breakthroughs you need.

These professional speakers and coaches dream of being world-class presenters. They need to present as often as they can. With social media "live" videos, they can turn on their cameras, and they have a stage. Knowing their dream and taking this challenge brought them all breakthroughs. Many of them were unexpected. They all grew because of their momentum.

So, I sat down and interviewed each of these emerging experts and asked some poignant questions about their challenges, breakthroughs and unexpected results. Look at what the daily commitment did for them. The 17-Minute Strategy works. I hope you are as inspired as I was when I heard about their breakthroughs.

KATHI KULESZA
KATHISPEAKS.COM

YOU ARE ALREADY A PROFESSIONAL SPEAKER. WHY JOIN THIS SEVENTY-SEVEN-DAY CHALLENGE?

I'm a "winger" of a speaker. And I do know that practicing, preparing, and thinking through your message is beneficial to us as speakers. I'm teaching somebody else's content as a contract trainer, and I want to be able to share my stories. So, for me, I feel like it gives me a chance to share my viewpoint and my content and prepare a little bit more. Some people are doing it to be more off-the-cuff, and I'm doing the challenge to be a little more intentional about my stories and what I'm sharing with the audience.

HOW HAS THE SEVENTY-SEVEN-DAY CHALLENGE HELPED YOU?

I would say one thing, because I have done it, is the commitment to do something every day—even on the days when you don't want to—because it gives you that momentum. I get a sense of accomplishment. It's the level of commitment. You do one thing every day for seventy-seven days and it gives you that momentum in your business and in your life.

HAS IT HELPED YOUR BUSINESS?

You don't know who is watching the videos when it's on your social media page. Then people reach out to you, and you think, "Oh, they're watching my videos? I guess I am reaching people." As a result of people watching my daily videos, I've reconnected with a couple people who will help me with a project I'm working on to determine how women can calculate their value as leaders. I connected with someone in HR who's going to be working on that project with me. I also got other podcast guest gigs as a result. So, every time you get to tell your story and talk about what you're sharing with the world, it gives you more exposure to other people's worlds.

WHAT WOULD YOU TELL SOMEONE CONSIDERING THE SEVENTY-SEVEN-DAY CHALLENGE?

I would say the fact that you're considering it means you have to do it. If you thought, "Maybe I should do that," that is your answer. Just do it, especially if your goal is to share your story and try to help people. If you feel like you have a message, a gift to give the world, you're doing a disservice by not doing it.

WHAT HAVE YOU LEARNED ABOUT YOURSELF THROUGH THIS PROCESS?

I've learned some of the stories that I talk about like they're no big deal are good stories with a message in them. I found that I can stick to something for seventy-seven days. Ironically, I was in the wellness business, and they say that seventy-five days is around the breaking point of New Year's resolutions where people quit them. So, making it seventy-seven days, we think we did it. They say about 75 percent of people quit their New Year's resolutions after seventy-five days. This came from the *Journal of Substance Abuse* in January 1988. They found that only 77 percent of resolvers kept their resolutions continuously for one week, 55 percent for one month, and only 19 percent at a two-year follow-up [https://www.researchgate.net/publication/223679624_The_resolution_solution_Longitudinal_examination_of_New_Year's_change_attempts].

ANYTHING ELSE IMPORTANT?

The other thing that I noticed that had a cool ripple effect is there are two people that I have relationships with outside of Stage Time University (Darren's online community) who started doing the challenge. One guy who's in wellness was already doing videos, but he adopted the Seventy-Seven-Day Challenge. He's two days ahead of us. Another friend of mine in the training industry and I started watching each other's videos besides watching everyone else's. So, you never know how your network is going to grow as a result of doing this.

Also, I did your daily video challenge a couple years ago, and through that, several of us doing the challenge started a mastermind group. That mastermind group teamed up and started doing an online summit of our own together as well. It's great to have people doing it with you because that motivates you to do the business and create a support network around you.

STEPHEN BOX
UNSHAKABLEHABITS.COM

WHY DID YOU DECIDE TO TAKE THE CHALLENGE?

The first thing I saw was day one of your challenge. I saw it the next day, and I was thinking, "What else am I doing right now?" To be honest, when I first started it, I didn't have any idea of this grand benefit that would come out of it. It was more of a why not. Why not just go ahead and challenge myself to something different and see what comes out of it?

WHAT DID YOU LEARN ABOUT YOURSELF DURING THE CHALLENGE?

For the first few days, I did some basic tip videos and had planned to do a bunch more, but I started to realize there was a real opportunity here to try new things, get clear on my message, and improve as a speaker. It was the first time in a while that I felt like I had permission to grow as a speaker.

One of the interesting things that happened within the first couple of days of the challenge made me start to have to think about the message that I was putting out into the world now that I'm having to take time every day to think about a story or lesson or some kind of tip that I want to share with people. I had to think about those and formulate them into a video. It forced me to get clear on the delivery of my message.

HOW DID YOU CONTINUE THE DAYS THAT YOU DIDN'T WANT TO?

There were a few days that I did not feel like doing it. I think the latest that I ever managed to squeeze my video in was at 11:50 p.m. I thought, "I have to do this to say that I still did it today." And the thing is, I teach people about creating unshakable habits. So, for me, this was an opportunity to practice what I preach. It was my chance to be committed on those days, especially on the days I was tired and didn't feel like doing it. I had long days because I had a lot of things going on in my personal life. I thought, "You know what? I committed to doing this. I'm going to be an example of what I preach." That was my motivation to keep going.

WHAT ARE SOME OF THE SIDE BENEFITS YOU DIDN'T ANTICIPATE?

When I first started it was more of an "Oh, let me do this to do it and see what happens" thing. And it didn't take long for me to start to say, "Maybe I can use this to build my audience, to build my business." But I didn't expect some of the feedback I've received from people. Being in Toastmasters for almost six years now, I'm used to feedback from people, but you're usually getting two to three minutes of feedback from one person. And what I found cool with this, especially with the Stage Time community, was multiple people were commenting and saying different things. And sometimes they would say the same thing in slightly different ways. So, I started getting information out of it.

For example, yesterday I did a video about what you do when what you know to do isn't working. The example that I used was based on my experience as a personal trainer. And even though that's only a small part of my business now, that's where I focused for that video. So, somebody commented, "Oh, you know, if you're trying to promote your personal training business, you should do the video from your gym." Duh. I realized my call to action didn't make it clear that I'm promoting something whole-health here. I'm going bigger than fitness. I need to make my call-to-action more clear. If I weren't getting that feedback from people daily, if I didn't have the opportunity to have hundreds of people give me feedback, I would have missed that. I want to continue doing videos and have a clearer call to action.

ANY OTHER BUSINESS BENEFITS FROM THE CHALLENGE?

Yes. First and foremost, I've gained a couple new clients out of it. The challenge has also given me a lot of clarity on where I wanted to take my business. My business was in a transition when I started the challenge. By getting on and doing the videos every day, I've gained a lot of clarity for myself about the direction that I wanted to take things, which has now opened up other opportunities because being clear about what I want to do makes it easier for me to know who I want to talk to. I've had several other members, also doing the challenge, reach out about setting up podcast interviews and things like that because they're watching my videos and like my message.

WHAT WOULD YOU SAY TO ANYONE CONSIDERING THE CHALLENGE?

There is something incredibly powerful about doing something consistently that requires you to get outside of your comfort zone. It requires you to think strategically about things randomly and be strategic in your approach. Over time, especially over a longer period of time, like seventy-seven days, if you're willing to experiment, if you're willing to play with it, you're willing to make mistakes and grow from them, the amount of growth that you can have in that time is crazy.

ANY OTHER INSIGHTS?

It's a lot of fun seeing your growth, and especially so if you have the opportunity to do it within a community where you can see the growth of others and provide each other with feedback, which is honestly one of the best ways to grow, because it occurs to you to grow from the feedback others receive, too. So, if you are going to do this, I encourage it. And if you have the opportunity to do it with other people, that will make it even better.

HOW WOULD YOU SUGGEST PEOPLE CREATE NEW HABITS?

What I've found that worked well for me was putting it on my calendar each day as a to-do item. I set mine as a notification for five minutes after I get up, and when it pops up on my phone, I do not swipe it away. It stares at me the entire day, saying, "Do your video." So, every time I opened Facebook, every time I checked a text, every time I wanted to go do anything on my phone, it was at the top of the screen, "Do your video." (For you, "Do your seventeen minutes!") Having that all-day reminder was helpful for me. Some people might also find attaching it to something you're already doing is helpful. That's one of the techniques I teach people. So, for example, I'm going to brush my teeth, and then I'm going to walk into my office, turn on my camera, do my video, or whatever the challenge is for you. You say, "I'm going to go do that right after I brush my teeth." So, it's a win-win; you get fresh breath, and you get stuff done.

AMANDA MAE GRAY
AMANDAMAEGRAY.COM

YOU ALREADY SEEM TO HAVE CONFIDENCE ON CAMERA; WHY DID YOU DO THE CHALLENGE?

One, I felt like I had to, and two, I felt like it was going to force me to get better at something I already felt comfortable and proficient in. So, I wanted to start a video podcast at some point, but I didn't have that great idea for it, which fueled it as well. My YouTube channel was stalling out, and I wasn't sure what to do with it. So I was thinking, "If I do this, it'll make me talk every single day, get more comfortable, make me be innovative, figure things out, and overall, get better at speaking on camera," which is ultimately what I want to do.

WHAT HAVE YOU LEARNED ABOUT YOURSELF IN THE PROCESS?

It's interesting because I think I said to you at one point that I'm not a motivational speaker. I want to be someday, but I don't know if that's my thing. It has forced me to talk about different ideas because, as you know, you think you have a few ideas at the beginning during the challenge, and then, eventually, you have to turn that camera on and start talking. You think, "I don't know what I'm going to say today, but it's 11:00 p.m., so, we're just going to turn on the camera and figure it out." And in doing so, I have inspired some other people to start the challenge, which I didn't anticipate. Now, I have a couple of people in my own Toastmasters district that are not part of Stage Time University that are also doing the challenge because they wanted to jump on board. They tried to get better at speaking. They saw where I started, and they saw how I was improving and wanted that for themselves.

WHAT HAVE THEY TOLD YOU? HAVE THEY GROWN AS WELL?

Absolutely. One ended up joining Stage Time. She saw what I was doing and was thinking about it for a while. I told her it was never going to be the right time. So, now was the right time. She joined and has been so grateful to expand her horizons and start being around other like-minded people who want more, pushing the boundaries, and becoming better themselves. Because, as you know, we are like the people who we surround ourselves with.

WHAT POSITIVE SIDE EFFECTS HAVE YOU EXPERIENCED?

I have started to interview other people, which I think is great. It's a good skill to learn. And especially if that's something I want to do as a podcast host. I've also been asked to be on a few other shows. People are even approaching me to be on my live with me even after the challenge ends, which is cool.

Other speakers have now recognized me as somebody who knows how to be on camera and set things up. So, they're asking me to help them with their setup, and I have now also been asked regularly to guest speak at other Toastmasters clubs.

And no, it's not paid yet, but it's all experience that will accumulate into what I know will be a successful career because I'm using this as a building block to create more and more.

PEOPLE LOVE YOUR ENERGY. YOU ARE CONFIDENT, SO WHY DO THIS?

Being good on camera was something I took for granted. I've been acting, modeling, and used to lights and cameras in front of my face for a long time. So, I was naturally good at it, but that doesn't mean I was good at formulating and using my own voice. Selling a product and being a promotional model, there's a script. There's a specific thing that I'm told, "Here are the guidelines. This is what you need to say." Finding your own voice and utilizing it and utilizing it effectively is completely different. So yes, I'm more comfortable on camera, but I didn't know how to put in structure. I didn't know the important things that I wanted to relay to other people. This challenge has shoved me into the deep end to find something important or useful to give back to other people. This experience will lead me to figure out my message.

WHAT WOULD YOU SAY TO SOMEONE CONSIDERING THIS CHALLENGE?

There's never going to be a right time. You need to do it. And don't hold yourself to a super high standard initially. First of all, this is not that hard. It is not. And the first time you're doing it, you're going to think it's hard. You're going to be nervous. It's going to be kind of on edge. Honestly, the first day I was thinking, "Oh man, now I got to do this thing." And I delayed a couple of days, which is why I'm a few days behind, and I did two, and then I took two days off and then came back.

So, you can do it—number one. Number two, it's not as hard

as you think it's going to be. And it's going to be innovation along your way. If you go back and look at my first video to where I am now with the setup and all the toys and the gadgets, it's night and day.

DO YOU THINK THE SEVENTY-SEVEN-DAY COMMITMENT IS IMPORTANT?

At first, the thought of seventy-seven days was like, "What are you talking about? That's crazy!" Right? Had I done seven days of this, I wouldn't be where I'm am now. Had I done 30 days of this, I wouldn't have innovated or grown nearly as much. I didn't start seeing the recognition or the opportunity or people saying things like, "Hey Amanda, we saw what you're doing, and we like it" from people responding who were past district directors and regional advisors in Toastmasters until at least fifty days in.

If it weren't a full seventy-seven days, the growth would not be as great. So yes, you could do a shorter one, but push yourself even more and see the growth. Because once you're at the end of the journey, you're going to be so grateful that you started it in the first place.

HOW HAS THE SEVENTY-SEVEN-DAY EXPERIENCE HELPED YOU (OR) BUILT YOUR BELIEF?

The seventy-seven-day challenge did two key things for me: it launched me into the world to be known as a thought leader, and it helped me stop overthinking my message and wording. Before, people saw me post here and there. They saw me make YouTube videos and give speeches, but I think it came across as more of a hobby, nothing serious. Now, people message me and comment about how I am inspirational to them, ask questions about my setup and how to do things, and see me overall as more of the pro. Additionally, I have learned that when I have a thought, I should put it out there. Not try to come up with the perfect wording or question if I should even say what I'm thinking publicly. I would talk myself out of acting more than taking the action. Overthinking has always been a struggle for me, and this has given me the confidence to think something through and then share it, to not try and be that perfect perception that no one wants to see anyway. I show up as me, the imperfect person, like everyone else.

FINAL THOUGHTS?

I started a podcast through this, and I don't know exactly what the name is. I'm currently using *Hello, Sunshine*, which was fun. And honestly, I have a pillow that says it. There you have it. But it's forced me into taking the idea that I had and implementing it. Even once the challenge is done, I might not do seven days a week, but I will be continuing to do lives and turning them into podcasts.

KORY MAY
STORYPROSPECTOR.COM

WHAT? YOU STARTED THE DAILY VIDEO CHALLENGE TWO YEARS AGO AND NEVER STOPPED?

I took the ninety-day public speaking challenge two years ago, and I went beyond ninety days. I went to a hundred days. Then I went to two hundred days and five hundred days. Now, last night I went to seven hundred nights consecutively of doing this ninety-day public speaking challenge.

WHY DID YOU START THE DAILY CHALLENGE?

I saw you do it. I saw Mark Brown, CSP, WCPS do it. I saw Albert Chang do it. I saw many Stage Time University folks doing it. I thought, "Well, if they can do it, I sure can." I started, and I stopped, and I didn't record anything, and I got butterflies. I was terrified. I was thinking, "I'm going to fall flat on my face, and ouch." The first one was the hardest. It was a eulogy for my high school choir teacher, and that got transmitted virally. My chorus teacher's family saw my eulogy and reached out and told me what a great job I had done touching them, and that gave me strength to do day number two. I moved into day number three, and it kept happening.

HOW HAS THIS DAILY CHALLENGE HELPED YOU?

There are a lot of ways in which this has helped me. First of all, it made me see the world in an entirely different way. Events happen to us every day. Storytellers are the ones that capture them, document them, and tell them again.

Second, it also forces you to write. I journal every day, and I'm constantly looking for stories. I'm listening for stories. I'm feeling for stories.

WHAT POSITIVE SIDE EFFECTS HAVE HAPPENED AS A RESULT?

I've become a better speaker. I've become a better listener. I've become a better thinker. All those things are happening because of the constant repetition of making that effort. As you say, investing your seventeen minutes a day is consistency. I am reminded of the book from Kobe Bryant, *The Mamba Mentality,* that people would see Kobe go into the gym and do his workout alongside him for two hours. But when he said, "Hey, I'm going to do that four hours, six hours, eight hours a day." at some point or another, not only did his natural talent takeover, but that work ethic enhanced and magnified whatever talent that he had. I feel that whatever talent that I've got has gotten a little better.

DID YOU GET ANY SPEAKING INVITATIONS AS A RESULT OF YOUR DAILY VIDEOS?

I've been asked to deliver keynotes in Mumbai and Kiev through Toastmasters. More importantly, it has helped me build friendships globally. And I appreciate that because business is one thing, but you can't have a business without people and personal relationships.

WHAT HAPPENS WHEN YOU DON'T FEEL LIKE DOING YOUR DAILY SEVENTEEN MINUTES?

The inner voice kicks in, saying, "Are you going to let the streak end? You can't let the streak end; come up with something." It's also deepened my faith because there's always something that needs to be said. When I don't think I have something to say, I close my eyes. I get centered, and something will appear.

WHAT WOULD YOU TELL SOMEONE WANTING TO BE BETTER AT DAILY VIDEOS?

First, relax. Second, breathe. Third, do it because you can't improve on something if you don't try. It's not about the first time. It's not even the second time, It is the accumulation of that effort and that energy that starts to help you see results.

I wouldn't have tried it if I hadn't seen you and Mark and Albert start and keep going. You give me courage.

ANYTHING ELSE?

First, my beliefs are strengthened by the thought that I can see and appreciate all of God's creation because that's where the stories are. Philippians 4:13: "I can do all things through Christ which strengthened me." This certainly lifted me along the way to over seven hundred nightly broadcasts.

Second, I'm using this challenge to discern who and what I am. I am a storyteller.

SARA MCGILL
RAISINGFEARLESSGIRLS.COM

ON A SCALE OF ONE TO TEN, WHAT DID YOU FEEL BEFORE YOUR FIRST VIDEO?

I was nervous, scared to be on camera and of being on live, of possibly making a mistake and saying the wrong thing. On a scale of one to ten, I was at twelve—maybe even fifteen. It was incredibly difficult for me to do that first video, but I did it.

HOW DID THE FIRST VIDEO GO?

I messed it up royally. It was awful, and everyone laughed, but nobody gave me a hard time about it. I purposely did not delete that first video. I wanted my daughters to see that I messed up and that it's okay to mess up.

The second day was slightly less difficult, but it was still hard knowing that I had to go back and do it again. And I thought, "Oh my God, I have another forty-nine to go." (Sara took a fifty-one-day video challenge.) It was a lot. And some days, I missed it, but not because I was scared (at least not after the first twenty videos). I did complete the challenge and went from this person who was incredibly self-conscious about how I appeared to others through that lens to being a person who knew that I had something good to say and good to share.

I got to the point where people were commenting and agreeing and saying, "Where did you get that?" because the videos were about my game-changers. Maybe it was about a product I use, something I enjoy, or something I do. And they would ask me questions about it. These people were interested in what I had to say.

Putting in those minutes every day, doing those little live videos, and sometimes they were longer live videos but doing that every day moved me toward being this person who was comfortable with myself and being seen through that lens by others. And that was huge.

WHAT GOT YOU TO COMMIT TO DOING THIS?

You did. And I had friends and mentors within Stage Time University who knew that I could do this, even though I thought, "There's no way." I have no desire to go live. I can do a speech that I have memorized and practiced, but just jump on a live video and talk to people? That was terrifying to me. I had other people who knew I could do it and had the faith that I could do it and said, "You just have to start."

WHAT POSITIVE SIDE EFFECTS OR BREAKTHROUGHS DID YOU EXPERIENCE?

I have a podcast, and I became more comfortable with it, especially the solo episodes that I do. Through my podcast, I also have a private Facebook group for girl moms. Within that group, I go live a lot. Sometimes I plan it. I think about what I'm going to say. I make notes. But most of the time, when I jump in there, it's because a thought pops into my head, and I think, "This is something my audience needs to know." So, I jump on and do a live video without a second thought. There's no way I could have done that if I had not done this challenge. I would have been tripping over my words. I was scared to say what I wanted to say and forgetting what I was supposed to say. But when you have conviction and when you've done these little videos, these little minutes, every day, you get to that point where you almost have to do it. You're comfortable doing it. You don't want to wait another minute. You think, "My audience needs to know this. I want to say it. I want to talk about it right now." And you do, and you can, because it becomes second nature.

WHAT WOULD YOU TELL SOMEONE NERVOUS ABOUT DOING THIS?

I don't think that anyone was more scared than I was. I screwed up royally on the first one. I thought I had hit the "stop record" button, but on Facebook, you have to hit two specific buttons. So, I hit the stop button, and I said, "Oh, God." And then I hit the second stop button, which finally stopped the live stream. And I thought, "Oh my God, was that on video?" It was, and everyone saw it—lots of people—because it was the very first time I had done a live video, which means it pops up in everyone's feed because of the Facebook algorithm.

So, everyone saw it. Everyone. But guess what? I didn't die. Nobody made fun of me. Yes, everyone laughed. Laughed with me, not at me. It gave me the courage to do it again the next day. I laughed about it then too. The next day, I said, "Hey, did you see yesterday's video? Go look because it was terrible, and I guarantee it'll make today's look even better." You have to have fun with it. Oh, and no one's going to make you do it. By hitting that "live" button, you make the choice, and you have to do it. The good news is you have the option of deleting it as soon as you finish or anywhere in the middle of your live speech. But I never did. Not for any of them because I wanted them all to be real and raw, mistakes and all.

HOW HAS THE SEVENTY-SEVEN-DAY EXPERIENCE HELPED YOU BUILD YOUR BELIEF?

I am a total believer in the seventy-seven-day challenge. Not only did I see myself grow from the challenge, but I watched all the other participants make huge strides in their speaking skills. The transformation I saw my peers make from timid and uncomfortable in the beginning to feeling confident and accomplished by the end was incredibly inspiring. And it took less than three months. It shows the real results of how big an impact can be by being consistent over such a little bit of time.

ALBERT CHANG
ALBERTCHANGSPEAKS.COM

WHY HAVE YOU DONE THE CHALLENGE THREE TIMES?

Initially, two years ago, when I saw the Ninety-Day Challenge, I said, "Oh, that's pretty cool." I saw other Stage Time members slowly starting and getting into it. At the time, I had no intention of doing it because I had never been on Facebook Live. And so, that was my mindset—watch everybody else do it. But then, slowly, I noticed even more members, one by one, started doing day one. And I thought, "Oh, okay. I'm feeling a little left out here." So, it was this indirect peer pressure that got to me. And one day, I decided, sitting in this same seat, late at night, and held up a phone and pressed "go live" in my pajamas. And that was it. I started from right there, even though I was uncomfortable. That was my whole message. That first one was getting comfortable being uncomfortable, and I battled through it. It became a lot easier as I progressed.

WHY DID YOU TAKE THE CHALLENGE A SECOND AND THIRD TIME?

So, after the challenge ended, especially the ninety-day one, that was it. There was nothing else done in that time period. Then, when the next challenge came, game changers, I'm thinking, "You know what? It's like, you're going to a gym, and you're strengthening and building this muscle." It's a skill to be able to go on these live videos. And because I hadn't done it for a while, I'm thinking, "I've got to go back to the gym. I have to get back into shape and strengthen that muscle even further." And it was the same thing this year with the seventy-seven-day challenge because of that gap. I felt like I lost something, and so I wanted to regain it. This time, I want to try to maintain it, instead of losing it again and regaining it in the future. So, it was more about maintaining that muscle and getting better each time out.

WHAT DID THE CHALLENGE TEACH YOU ABOUT YOU?

The biggest takeaway is that no matter what you want to achieve in life, it's always going to take getting uncomfortable, getting down deep into the weeds and battling through. If you want to improve a certain skill that you see others have, you, yourself, have to do some of the dirty work, and I shouldn't say suffer through it, but get uncomfortable and do it. And that's something that time and time again I'm applying to parts, whether I'm doing speeches or not, having to go through those coaching calls and again, having to dig deep and get uncomfortable through certain moments, so that I can come out of it stronger.

DID YOU EXPERIENCE ANY POSITIVE SIDE EFFECTS?

I had the experience of doing the past two challenges, and I was taking this other boot camp, this other course about how to pitch to television. And the homework that the instructors gave us was not to type things out in the private Facebook group. They told all the students, "Hey, we want to see you go on Facebook Live and verbalize this homework." And the majority of the class had never done a Facebook Live before. And so, for me, because I had the experience, I was able to articulate my ideas a little better than some of the other students. I knew how much the other students were like, "Oh, no." They were scared as well. I was glad to provide them the support at the same time, just to keep going, and to let them know that it's going to get better.

And throughout this process, because I was able to articulate my ideas a little more comfortably, I was able to make great connections with people I didn't expect to meet and keep in contact with them to this day. I just had someone up here as my first guest on my podcast because I was able to meet her through this boot camp. She was commenting on my Facebook posts within the group about the subject area that I spoke about. Thanks to these Facebook Live videos, I was able to post one right away with content that flowed nicely. And it was articulate without having to struggle through it.

HOW DID YOU HANDLE DAYS YOU DIDN'T WANT TO DO THE CHALLENGE?

I had done the challenge the past two years, so I was at the point where I thought this time I should narrow my focus onto certain subject areas. And it wasn't as plentiful. I had topics I

could talk about, but it wasn't necessarily related to my subject area. So I would look at my list of notes on all the topics
I talked about, to make sure I'm not repeating myself, and I'd
think, "Oh, I don't have anything to talk about." I didn't want to
do something random for the sake of the challenge and speak
without a purpose for my audience. So those were the days I
didn't want to do the challenge.

Then I got to thinking, "You know what? If Kory May's doing
a thousand days in a row right now, I shouldn't be sitting here
doing nothing." I have no excuses, and I want to get back and
just finish it off and then keep going because he's out there doing
this nonstop. And I see other people being motivated by what he
did, going beyond the seventy-seven days. So, why not? And no
matter what, even though there are days I don't want to do it, if
he can do it, then I think we all can do it too. That's what I'm
going to do—take it to the end.

HOW HAS THE CHALLENGE HELPED YOU GROW?

These challenges have given me a rough draft of content that
I can repurpose and reuse eventually because I'm building an
inventory of ideas that I can use later. Whether I clean it up, do
it more formally, and make YouTube videos, or whether it goes
into future podcast episodes, or it's part of a course I create, I'm
able to at least get it out there. I've been trying to write a book
for the last two years, and I'm essentially creating content by
doing these videos, so I don't have to start from scratch. I can
always refer back to all the videos that I've done and now incor-
porate them into the book. I need to work on an outline, and
I'll be able to fill in the key areas more easily with any content
that I've created.

WHAT WOULD YOU TELL SOMEONE CONSIDERING THE CHALLENGE?

I get it. There's always that fear of trying something new, and it's normal. That feeling of fear means you're human and it's expected, but once you get through that first one, once you power through it, it will get a lot easier each time out. And I would say start simple; take the easiest lesson that you've learned. If you want to do it for less than a minute, so be it, as long as you're able to put yourself out there that one time, just once. From that point on, you're going to be able to take off and fly.

WHERE ELSE IN YOUR LIFE HAS DOING THE CHALLENGE HELPED YOU?

So, because the theme is about getting uncomfortable and moving through the discomfort, that process can benefit me somehow in many areas. I've always had a fear throughout my life because I'm more introverted, I'm more reserved, and I'm not the most outgoing person. And so, I was a shy kid growing up. And all these experiences, including doing these live videos of shattering that barrier and putting myself out there, have helped me overcome the fear of reaching out to strangers that I have always had. And it's helped me out in my professional career where I might feel intimidated in approaching some of the higher-ups within my company because I need to talk to them about my work, trying to see if they can help me out with certain things in terms of, "Hey, can you support me in getting a promotion?"

Or to ask, "Can you write me a nice feedback?" Because usually, I would be like, "Okay, okay. I don't want to bother this person at all." But now I'm more freely able to reach out to whomever I need to—no matter what level they are, even the higher-up directors within my company. And yeah, that fear still exists, but I'm more able to do it with less hesitation. And if there's something that I need that's important, reaching out and asking has become a lot easier because I'm putting myself through experiences where it is uncomfortable. And the more I do that, the more I can do it in other areas of life.

HOW IMPORTANT WAS DOING THE CHALLENGE FOR SEVENTY-SEVEN DAYS?

Having a number like seventy-seven, sure, it might seem challenging, and that's what you want; you need a challenge, if you wanted the satisfaction of achieving. But it's not like it's a hundred, two hundred, where people will be thinking, "Oh my goodness, how am I going to do this?" No, there's that sense that it's doable. But, and on the other side, it's not so short where you're not going to strengthen that muscle. So, it's a great balance where it's long enough that you are going to grow. You are going to strengthen yourself. You're going to gain skills along the way, but it's not hugely impossible either, as well, that you might think to yourself at first, "Nah, no," with an attitude of giving up right away before you even started.

And so, that's what you need. You need a certain duration where you can have real growth. You might not notice it at first, but when you've done the challenge and you go back and watch the first video and watch that last video, you will see something that's night and day. Doing it for seventy-seven days is that perfect zone where you will see that growth visually, even though you might not feel like it during the process. In the end, it's there. Doing it for seventy-seven days is necessary for you to get to that point.

HOW DID YOU TRANSFORM BECAUSE OF THE CHALLENGE?

I transformed in the sense that I'm open to trying new things more than ever. And because I'm more open, I never know what opportunities and benefits that I might receive. For example, if it weren't for this challenge, as I mentioned, I wouldn't have made those connections in that other boot camp that I had taken. If it weren't for taking this challenge two years ago, I wouldn't have been part of this mastermind with other Stage Time members with Tim, Bob, and Kathi. It's because of taking the opportunities presented to me and being more open-minded that I was able to benefit from it. Now, if any other challenges lie ahead of me, I'm more open-minded to trying them, because who knows what kind of benefits they could lead to?

ANY WORDS OF WISDOM?

I would have to say, seventeen minutes, or committing to a timeframe every day and doing these challenges, at least, gives you that committed timeframe. And who knows what's going to come out of your mind from trying it because understandably, there are people who are starting this challenge. They don't know what it is, what their voice is, at the time, but if you're not able to get it out there and freely practice, it's never going to come out. Sometimes during the challenges, there were days where I had planned a certain topic, but something else popped into my mind last minute. And that's the topic that I'd go with at that moment when I'm going on Facebook Live. And I'm thinking at the end, "Oh, thank goodness I got that on tape somewhere."

And so, doing these challenges, at least, gets your thoughts and your ideas out into the open because the more you can get it out, the more you can refine it. And the more you can go back to it and use it later on. And if you're keeping it inside of you, you might forget about it.

You could be helping somebody out there who needs to hear your message. That's the common theme I learned with everybody here at Stage Time and all the faculty: Who knows who your audience is, and what they will be getting from you when you speak?

WHAT KIND OF COMMENTS HAVE YOUR DAILY VIDEOS BEEN GETTING?

Throughout these challenges, I've heard from people that I haven't seen in years, and out of the blue, they are commenting on these live videos, saying, "Wow," and "Oh my goodness, I had no idea you could speak so well." They're so shocked and amazed and some of them get entertained with some of the thoughts that I have daily. A lot of it has been positive and a lot of them, like any of the topics that I talk about, will say, "Yeah, yes. I think the same way about what you're talking about." It has been overwhelmingly positive. It's great to reconnect with people that I haven't talked with or seen in decades. That's been my experience in doing these live videos over the last two years now.

CHAPTER 19

YOUR NEXT CHAPTER

THE BOOK IS over? Already?

Yep.

I could have written a longer book, but I'd rather you start your minutes. If you want more value from this book, reread it. That would give you twice the value. You didn't buy this book to have another book to read. You bought it because there is a dream inside you that needs to come to life or be resuscitated. Since you're not dead, you're not done. You're still alive, and you have a second chance. You may not get a third. *Go all-in.*

What if I'm right? What if this could work for you?

Often, I recall those words of Brian Tracy I previously shared: "What would you dare to dream if you knew you wouldn't fail?" In my head, I answered, "I'd be a comedian. I'd make people laugh for a living." I decided I had to commit to trying it at least once.

REGRETS SUCK.

I could live with bombing one time in front of a group of strangers. I could not live with the regret of wondering, "What if Brian Tracy was right?" That would haunt me. That I could not live with.

As of the time of publishing this book, I have not yet sold my script. I'm still doing my seventeen minutes. If you want to see my struggle go check out #17MinuteChallenge or go to 17MinutesToYourDreams.com.

Remember my little CD celebrations? In 2019, when I hit that financial low because I was not paying attention to my bottom line, I had to sell those CDs on Offer Up. I think I got $40 for fifty CDs, which bought a lot of mac and cheese. Do what you need to do. I took a few minutes to reflect on what they meant. They served their purpose. They brought me meaning when I needed it. Then I let them go. You may have to let go of a few things and people along the way to get to where you want to be.

Remember the promise I made to God that He could use me however He wanted? Well, this book was an inspired thought for sure. It was something I just *had* to do. There was no contemplation. When I sat down, it flowed out. I wrote it in seventeen days. I believe it was a God-nudge to write it. I know it was for someone. Maybe it was written just for you?

Critical:

Some minutes will give you *hope.*

Some minutes will give you *progress.*

All minutes will give you *momentum.*

How do you start the next chapter in your dream? You have *all-in intelligence*:

THREE All-In Steps

1. Make the choice (You are the C.E.O).

2. Start the habit (Do your seventeen minutes).

3. Get two accountability buddies (Gain momentum).

You don't know which minutes will matter.

I'll end this book with three of the lines from my world championship speech:

> *I was not given the gift of making people laugh; I was given the opportunity to take the next step.*
>
> *What's your next step?*
>
> *Take it.*

(See the 77-Day Challenge Tracker on Page 165)

CONGRATULATIONS! BAM! DID YOU GET BREAKTHROUGHS?
#17MINUTECHALLENGE

Start your 77-Day-Challenge Tracker
spreadsheet or download mine.
Go to:
17MinutesToYourDream.com/download

LOVE THE 17 MINUTES STRATEGY?

Inspire your whole team to take the challenge and
experience the breakthroughs they desire.

If you'd like more information about bulk order discounts
please email support@stagetimeuniversity.com or call
1-888-828-4451.

GOT PRESENTATIONS?

Where Good Presenters Become
UNFORGETTABLE!

Go to: StageTimeUniversity.com

Want a Daily Dose of
Inspiration?

Get Paid to Speak!
Highly-paid speakers aren't lucky; They're trained.

Do you want to...?
√ **Get More Bookings**

√ **Get Higher Fees**

√ **Build Your Business**

If Your Message Matters, We Help You Find Your Audience So They Love You & You Get Paid to Deliver it

It begins with our 59-minute training, no charge.
In this free training, you'll get 3 secrets:

#1: Find out what clients really pay for. (Hint: It's not a speech.)

#2: YOU don't need big credentials to get big fees.

#3: Marketing is always changing, so get in the loop!

To learn more, visit:
GetPaidtoSpeakTraining.com

APPENDIX

ACKNOWLEDGMENTS

THIS BOOK WOULD not have come to be if it weren't for:

God, who spoke through me and allowed this book to pour out of me in seventeen days.

Thank you, Mom and Dad, for allowing this broke dreamer, who had massive school loans and a business loan but no business, to live at home with and charged me next-to-nothing rent. Your unconditional love is what allowed me to pursue the seemingly impossible. I'm sure after helping put me through business school, then coping with the thought of your naïve, shy, introverted son dreaming of being on stage, inspiring people through laughter must have made your head spin like a cartoon character. I'm truly sorry for the stress I caused you. I hope you know that the tens of thousands of people around the world I've touched started with you and your love. I'll forever remember your wisdom, Dad, when you said, "I don't care what you want to be, just be the best." We did it.

To my team: Mark Brown, Regine Hollenbeck, Ed Tate,

Craig Valentine, Dawson Antonucci, Patti Marler, Martina Krebsbach, Mike Davis, Jennifer Leone, Stephanie McHugh, Kevin Burke and Zoey.

To the people who came alongside me: Vince Antonucci, Jim Stovall, Michael Hauge, Michael Starr, Maureen Zappala, Mike Rayburn, Marilyn Sherman, Jennifer Joseph Lier, Suzy Dickstein, Sara Ivie, Butch Bradley, and Fredrick.

My own students, whose courage and breakthroughs inspired me that this needed to be a book: Kathi Kulesza, Sara McGill, Amanda Mae Gray, Albert Chang, Stephen Box, Kory May, and Chic Miller.

Also, thanks to Henry DeVries, Devin DeVries, Andy Baird, Lisa Haney, Edie DeVilbiss, Rich Hopkins, Paula Tomko, Tanya Murray, Manuela Braun Hendrickson, Liza Richards, Ashley Morris, and Katherine Wertheim.

ABOUT THE AUTHOR

He felt invisible in high school.
He failed as a business owner.
He worked in a cubicle for over a decade.
Today, he's a world champion speaker.
What made the difference for him can
make the difference for you.

DARREN LaCROIX'S JOURNEY is a real-life underdog story filled with humor and hope.

After a failed business in 1992, Darren took a dare and took the stage at an open-mic night at a Boston comedy club. He bombed miserably. It was horrible. The headliner that night told him, "Don't quit your day job, kid." Friends told him that his dream of making people laugh for a living was crazy and stupid. He didn't listen.

He may have been born without a funny bone in his body,

but Darren possessed the desire to learn and the willingness to fail. This self-proclaimed student of comedy is living proof that *anything* can be learned.

Less than nine years later, in 2001, Darren outspoke 25,000 contestants from fourteen countries to become the Toastmasters International World Champion of Public Speaking. Ironically, it was with a funny speech. Some said it was one of the best speeches in the history of the contest.

Since that victory, he has delivered keynotes in every state in the United States and forty-four international cities. He is passionate about showing people that if you pray, find the right mentors, and become a sponge, anything is possible.

Darren is currently the only speaker in the world who is a CSP (Certified Speaking Professional), an AS (Accredited Speaker), and a World Champion of Public Speaking. Despite this, Darren always reminds people, "The letters after your name are not as important as the professional you become in the process."

He is the cohost of *Unforgettable Presentations* podcast. Through his live workshops and StageTimeUniversity.com, he helps good presenters become *unforgettable*.

SEVENTY-SEVEN-DAY CHALLENGE TRACKER
#17MINUTECHALLENGE

Day	Date	Mins Today	Mins Total	What I Did Today	Any Breakthroughs?
1					
2					
3					
4					
5					
6					
7					
8					
9					
10					
11					
12					
13					
14					
15					
16					
17					
18					

19				
20				
21				
22				
23				
24				
25				
26				
27				
28				
29				
30				
31				
32				
33				
34				
35				
36				
37				
38				

#17MINUTECHALLENGE Start your 77-Day-Challenge Tracker spreadsheet or download mine. Go to 17MinutesToYourDream.com/download.

39					
40					
41					
42					
43					
44					
45					
46					
47					
48					
49					
50					
51					
52					
53					
54					
55					
56					
57					
58					

#17MINUTECHALLENGE Start your 77-Day-Challenge Tracker spreadsheet or download mine. Go to 17MinutesToYourDream.com/download.

59				
60				
61				
62				
63				
64				
65				
66				
67				
68				
69				
70				
71				
72				
73				
74				
75				
76				
77				

#17MINUTECHALLENGE Start your 77-Day-Challenge Tracker spreadsheet or download mine. Go to 17MinutesToYourDream.com/download.

Made in the USA
Middletown, DE
09 March 2022

62323881R00111